The
Downtown
Girl's Guide
to Wine

The Downtown Girl's Guide to Wine

How to Buy, Serve, and Sip
with Style and Sophistication

Megan Buckley and Sheree Bykofsky

Adams Media
Avon, Massachusetts

Published by
Adams Media, an F+W Publications Company
57 Littlefield Street, Avon, MA 02322. U.S.A.
www.adamsmedia.com

ISBN: 1-59337-351-1

Printed in Canada.

J I H G F E D C B A

Library of Congress Cataloging-in-Publication Data
Buckley, Megan.
The downtown girl's guide to wine / Megan Buckley and Sheree Bykofsky.
p.   cm.
Includes bibliographical references.
ISBN 1-59337-351-1
1. Wine and wine making. I. Bykofsky, Sheree. II. Title.

TP548.B895 2005
641.2'2--dc22
2005019806

This publication is designed to provide accurate and authoritative information with
regard to the subject matter covered. It is sold with the understanding that the pub-
lisher is not engaged in rendering legal, accounting, or other professional advice.
If legal advice or other expert assistance is required, the services of a competent
professional person should be sought.

—From a *Declaration of Principles* jointly adopted by a
Committee of the American Bar Association and a
Committee of Publishers and Associations

Many of the designations used by manufacturers and sellers to distinguish their
product are claimed as trademarks. Where those designations appear in this book
and Adams Media was aware of a trademark claim, the designations have been
printed with initial capital letters.

This book is available at quantity discounts for bulk purchases.
For information, please call 1-800-872-5627.

*For Karen Buckley, who told me
to write the $%^!&£! book
because it's what I was meant to do.*

~ MB

Contents

Acknowledgments

Katharine Sands, the godmother of our second book; Karen Hassey, best friend and "research assistant" extraordinaire, without whom Megan would have drowned in a vat of Gewürztraminer; Jill Alexander, friend, fabulous editor, and the funniest person I know, who believed in this book first; Gary Krebs, Kirsten Amann, copyeditor Susan Aufheimer, technical reviewers Misty Kalkofen and Jackson Cannon, and everyone else associated with Adams who helped this book come to be; Pat Buckley, who needs to put more water in his bourbon; Dan Buckley, who likes Colt 45; Craig and Toni Boelsen of Camp Boelsen for Wine Lovers; Gene Anne and Kelly Smith, who tell Megan when she's gained weight and who pour her a Guinness when it's much needed; Barbara Campbell; Janet Rosen, always famous because she's not a man; Erin Sullivan, always there to listen and talk sense into the wayward; Toni Leonard, Consultant of Cool; Tim McDonnell and all the folks at East of Eighth; Brian McKay, who has a Ph.D. in the art of the pickup line; Gwendolyn Wilson, Lee Fleming, Ian Mendelsohn, and all the amazingly knowledgeable, helpful wine experts who answered—or offered to answer—our questions; Lori Perkins, who always has a plan; Brian Rubin, who can talk anyone down from a tree; Denis and Kevin Fitzgerald and everyone at Fitzgerald's Pub, always a safe haven for a beer break; Susan Bakos (or "Auntie Suze"); Liz Wagenschutz, Meatloaf lover and friend from afar; Stephany Evans, who can always be counted on to go for a glass of wine. What would we have done without you all?!

—MB, SB

Introduction

Wine. That stuff that comes in bottles, jugs, or boxes. It's made from grapes. They serve it at church. You also hear that it might be good with food. And since it's got alcohol, it's definitely good for lowering those pesky inhibitions. Right?

Well, yes and no! In fact, make that a resounding *no!* There's so much more to the world of wine than that. You certainly don't have to be a wine snob (or a snob of any kind!) to enjoy it. And the best part: The way to learn about wine, aside from reading this book, is by doing a lot of (responsible) drinking!

Yeah, we know it seems so much easier to just order a Cosmo, an apple martini, or a mojito, and skip the wine list altogether. That's what we thought in our PWL (Pre-Wine-Loving) era. As you'll see in the pages to come, although we're huge proponents of the Drink What You Like theory, we're even bigger champions of the Try a Lot of Stuff movement. We, too, love a good frozen margarita with salt, a perfectly poured piña colada, a decadent chocolate martini, or even the occasional Long Island iced tea, but nothing, and we mean nothing, can replace vino. Why? Because it engages all of your senses. (Except hearing. Although if you put your ear to a glass of freshly poured sparkling wine, you'll be able to hear the bubbles popping on the surface!)

Wine comes in a range of colors that delight the eyes, from a yellow so pale it's almost clear to reds so deep they're almost black. And if you stick your nose into a glass of white wine, you might smell passion fruit, flowers, freshly cut grass, or bananas, just to name a few. Sniff a glass of red, and perhaps you'll get a nose full of smoke, spices, fresh red fruit, earth, or dried cherries. And then there's taste! White wines can taste like honey, minerals, citrus fruits, and much more, while reds can smack of black pepper, dark red fruit, even coffee, chocolate, or licorice. You won't want to stick your fingers in your wine to feel its texture, but you'll be able to feel it on your tongue, whether it's thick and rich, like a dessert wine, or light and bubbly, like a sparkling wine. It's true: Wine can give you a sensual, full-body experience!

Which is not to say that wine's superserious. No way! While wine is indeed an art and a science, it's also a beverage that's made to be enjoyed. And enjoying it can be a blast. We can't count the number of times one of us has jumped up from our seat after trying a new wine, exclaiming, "Oh my gosh, it tastes like bananas!" or "Wow, it really smells like tobacco!" or "I can't believe it! It *does* smell like breakfast pastries!"

That's the spirit in which we've written *The Downtown Girl's Guide to Wine*. In the fun-filled chapters to follow, we'll give you the skinny on the grapes (and the wines made from them) you've heard about, but can't quite define. You'll also get the scoop on some great grapes and their wines that you might not recognize, but that are so delicious, you'll want to run right out and try them yourself. And we'll fill you in big-time on which wines are hot around the world.

But wait, ladies, that's not all! We'll also give you tips for throwing a wine-and-cheese party, for planning a hedonistic Champagne-and-chocolate soiree that'll make you the toast of the town, for making your own wine charms (a fun way to dress up any wineglass!), and tons more. Plus, since wine with food is a classic combo, we'll show you how to order wine in a restaurant without feeling stupid, and we'll toss you a few hints about food and wine pairing. Oh, and look for useful-in-a-pinch hangover tips, quirky quotes, ideas for what to wear when you're sipping your favorite glass of vino, and anecdotes on what *not* to do when you're imbibing. (We learned the hard way, so you don't have to!)

We aren't sommeliers, winemakers, or bar owners. We're just a couple of Downtown Girls who love nothing more than kicking off our stilettos and relaxing with a couple glasses of great wine.

Megan Buckley and Sheree Bykofsky,
September 2005

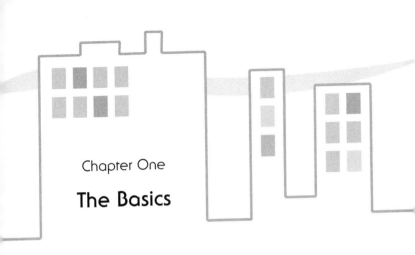

Chapter One

The Basics

Wine makes daily living easier, less hurried, with fewer tensions and more tolerance.

—*Benjamin Franklin*

So you've probably asked yourself (or maybe someone's asked you!), what *is* wine? And perhaps you're stumped. With the aura of mystery and complexity that surrounds wine, you probably—and with good reason—assume it's something as easy to grasp as, say, the Holy Grail or why we all loved *Dawson's Creek* with undying passion.

Well, here's a surprise: Wine is nothing but fermented grape juice. That's right. When you get that glass of Chardonnay or Merlot or Blaufränkisch at a wine bar, you're drinking nothing but fermented grape juice. Hypothetically, you could even make wine in your bathtub. (But girls, please don't try that at home. At least not in the bathtub. Gross.)

Yes, wine is that simple—but it's also complex. Because winemaking is a lot more than stomping on grapes à la Lucy Ricardo. Wine may just be fermented grape juice, but the taste, style, and quality of the wine depends on everything from the character of the grape; where that grape is grown; how rainy or dry the season was that year; how much sunlight the grapes got; how long the skins on the grapes were left to soak in the juice after the grapes were pressed; whether the wine was aged in barrels made of new oak, old oak, or steel; and so much more. But in general, it's safe to say that the way a wine tastes is determined by three conditions: the variety of the grape the wine's made from; the *terroir* (pronounced tear-WAH, French for "earth"), which refers to the general environment in which the grape was grown, including the soil, the weather, the altitude at which it grew; and the winemaking process.

Whew. Don't get bogged down by all those variables. Just know this: Like people, flowers, and that one-of-a-kind bag you managed to snag for $10 at a sample sale, no two wines are alike. The differences are what makes wines exciting, and worthy of obsession by wine critics and fools alike.

That said, before we dig in (or drink in, rather), here's the short version of how wine is made. Keep in mind that saying, "This is how wine is made, in a nutshell" is like saying, "Let me tell you my life history—including my four exes, my childhood in the Amazon, and why I have a penchant for things that are pink—in just a sentence or two."

All wine is made by crushing grapes and then placing the mash in some sort of closed container, usually a huge barrel made of wood or steel, and letting the grape mash ferment (that is, letting the natural sugar in the grapes turn into alcohol). But what makes a wine red or white? (For that matter, what makes so many women think Hugh Jackman looks hot with lamb-chop sideburns in *X-Men*?) Black grapes are used to make red wine. Their skins are so dark they look black, but when crushed, the skins give the wine a red pigment. The winemaker allows the grape skins to macerate (soak) in the grape juice. The longer the skins remain in the juice, the darker the wine will be. If the skins hang out in the juice for only a few hours, you end up with pink, or rosé, wine. And if the grapes are pressed so carefully that the skins don't break and have no contact with the juice—wham! White wine from red grapes. Blood from a stone. Anything's possible!

You can also make white wine from white grapes. Whether the skins are allowed to touch the juice or not, the wine will still be white. (Actually, it'll be yellow. Take a look at that glass of Chardonnay. By Jove! White wine is not white at all.)

As for sparkling wine: No, the winemaker doesn't mix Sprite with Sauvignon Blanc. (And no sparkling wine should taste like that, either!) After the grape juice ferments (by letting the yeast and sugar in the juice turn into alcohol) and turns into wine, the winemaker adds more yeast and sugar to it and lets the wine ferment *again*. That's what produces the bubbles that make the wine, well, sparkle.

And lastly, fortified wines are wines with alcohol added—often in the form of brandy. These wines, such as port or sherry, are meant for drinking in relatively small quantities. (Same goes for dessert wines like the fabulous German Eiswein, which has no extra booze added to it, incidentally). They're potent, often sweet, and they can have up to twice the alcohol of table wines. So sip with care!

Demystifying the Wine Label: Those Fancy Words Aren't There Just to Look All Eurotrashy

You're standing in a liquor store, eyes glazed over in confusion at the scores and scores of wines, many from France, Germany, Italy, and loads of other countries around the world—and it's all Greek to you. (Sometimes the label really *is* in Greek—especially if you're looking at a Greek wine.) Try not to get frustrated and grab the first $3.99 bottle of Merlot you see. Here's a general breakdown—and explanation—of some of the information you, Ms. Savvy Wine Buyer, can glean from the information on the label alone. We've all made the mistake of judging a wine by its pretty label; remember, a striking, well-designed label doesn't guarantee you'll be getting a good wine!

Wines are named after either the place where the grapes are grown or the type of grape the wine's made from. In Old-World countries—that is, many European countries, especially in France, wines tend to be named for the places the grapes are grown, not for the grapes from which the wines are made. So it'll take a little learning on your part to know, say, which grapes are used to make a Côtes du Rhône.

What else can you learn from a label? It also lists the producer, the name of the importer, and a standard government warning that alerts people to the risks of consuming alcohol. Most European countries, such as France, Italy, Germany, Spain, and Portugal, have laws controlling the quality of their wines (a very good thing!). Wines of the best quality in these countries sport the abbreviations AOC or AC (in France), DOC (in Italy and Portugal), DOCa (in Spain), or QbA (in

Germany). These abbreviations stand for, in their respective languages, "controlled" or "regulated" names of regions. They certify you're getting a wine that meets certain government-mandated benchmarks. The label will read something like this: "Appellation Côtes du Rhône Côntrolée." Although the abbreviations won't guarantee you'll get la crème de la crème, so to speak, you can safely assume that the wine you buy won't be total swill. See, when it comes to reading European wine labels, it pays to read the fine print!

> *Eat your bread with gladness,*
> *and drink your wine with a merry heart.*
> *—Ecclesiastes 9:7*

"New World" refers to any non-European country that produces wine, including the United States, Australia, New Zealand, Chile, and Argentina. Most New-World wines are named after the grape from which they are made. The large type on the label usually reads something like this: Cherry Pop, Cabernet Sauvignon. You're not drinking a wine called Cherry Pop (though a grape worthy of that name does sound tasty!); you're drinking a Cabernet made by Cherry Pop Winery, otherwise known as the producer. Then they'll mention the part of the country or the state where the wine was made, and the vintage (the year the grapes were harvested), which might read, "California, 2003." For our purposes, pay minimal attention to the vintage. The vast majority of wines you'll be buying are meant to be drunk within a year or so, not aged. The only other way the vintage is useful is if you happen to know that 2003 was a great year for, say, most Long Island Gewürztraminers. But if you know that kind of thing for most winemaking regions in the country, you probably don't need this book!

In very small type, in a corner of the label, you'll see the alcohol content (it's usually not less than 9 percent or more than 14 percent). Turn the bottle around, and you'll see a second label sporting the government-mandated warning about alcohol consumption, a couple of sentences about the wine (which may or may not be accurate), and where the wine was bottled.

How to Taste Wine— No Spitting, Slurping, or Funny Faces Necessary!

The great thing about wine is, it requires attention. You can't appreciate its full value by slugging it back, so please, don't treat it like a vodka tonic, a draft of light beer, or an energy drink—because that's no fun at all! Wine engages all of your senses. Think of it as meditation—except it tastes a lot better.

Look at the wine. Swirl it around in the glass to aerate it, and its fragrance opens up. One easy way to aerate your wine without spilling it is to set the glass on a flat surface, slide the stem of the glass between your index and middle fingers and press down on the base of the glass. Then move the glass side to side. It's a nice, discreet way to swirl the wine and it shows you know what you're doing. Then sniff it. Stick your nose right into the glass—don't worry about being delicate or screwing up your makeup. You won't. (Unless you're a chronic "nose wetter" like Megan, who continually manages to plunge her entire nose into the wine. If that happens to you, just laugh, dab your nose off with a napkin, and crack a dumb joke or two. Works like a charm.) Keep sniffing for a full sixty seconds. What do you smell? Spice? Chocolate? A twenty-dollar bill? It's like that toucan in the commercial for a fruity, sugary cereal popular in the eighties: Your nose always knows.

And remember, the only person tasting that glass of wine in front of you is you. (Unless, of course, you decide to share.) Which means that whatever you see, smell, taste, and feel in a sip of wine is correct. There are no wrong answers, kids—and don't let anyone tell you otherwise!

Okay, at this point we have a sneaking suspicion that you're asking, do they actually put citrus fruit, cracked black pepper, or wet dog into the wine to achieve these aromas? Don't be embarrassed. It's something we ruminated on for years without ever having the courage to ask. But the answer is, hell no. The exceptions (such as a wonderful blueberry juice–infused Champagne produced at a winery in New Jersey) are as few and far between as there are decent guys at a frat party. Here's the amazing thing: The chemical makeup of the aromas the wine gives off are, somehow, very similar to the aromas given off by the real thing, whatever it may be. Okay, so how do these aromas actually get in the wine? It's complex, and to explain the whole thing would require vast scientific knowledge. For our purposes, the science really isn't important. The short answer is that it has to do with the terroir (environment) the grapes for the wine are grown in. Essences of the surrounding environment get into the air, water, and soil surrounding the grapes. Thus, if wild mushrooms grow in close proximity to the grapes, or the air is infused with the scent of lavender, more likely than not, those essences will leave their imprint on the flavor of the grape—and the wine. Just remember that scents of chocolate, for example, don't come from putting chocolate in the wine.

Now, as our friend Bill Shakespeare once said, it's time to "give to airy nothing / A local habitation and a name." While scores of different aromas are given off by wine, you can generally bet a lifetime supply of Lulu Guinness handbags that most of what you smell can be placed in the following categories: floral, fruity, herbaceous, mineral, earthy, animal, vegetable, or off-putting. An off-putting smell is a bad thing in wine. Such a wine might taste like, well, rotten eggs, or a dead mouse stuck in the power strip under the desk for a few months. Seriously. The smell might be the result of a bad cork, storing the wine at wildly wrong temperatures, or God knows what else. You probably won't encounter too many off-putting wines (hopefully), but when you do, feel free to take it back to the shop where you purchased it, or, if you're at a restaurant, politely ask the waiter for a new bottle.

On to what you *should* be tasting! To help you make sense of it all, here's a brief list of aromas you might smell and the categories they fall into:

- Floral—well, flowers; think roses, violets, carnations
- Fruity—blackberry, plum, cherry, red currant, black currant (usually in red wine), apricot, citrus (lemon and lime), pear, kiwi, lychee, green apple (usually in white wine)

- Herbaceous—grass, basil, rosemary, anise (or black licorice), vanilla
- Earthy—mushrooms, truffles (not the chocolate kind!), soil, wet leaves, a forest
- Animal—wet dog, a barnyard, leather, wet wool, beeswax, fur
- Vegetable—asparagus, green pepper, tobacco, dry leaves
- Spice—pepper, cinnamon, nutmeg, roasted nuts

Now, take a sip of the wine. You may have seen wine aficionados make quite a show of slurping it up, swooshing it around in their mouths and practically gargling it like it's Listerine, all the while looking, well, strange. What could pass for the mating rituals of tropical birds actually do have a noble purpose, but we've learned that you can be discreet about tasting wine and still get the proper effect.

When you're tasting a wine, take a medium-size sip, one that's more than enough to wet your tongue, but not so much that your cheeks are bulging like a drunk

How Do You Get Red Wine Stains Out of Clothes?

Don't despair; your favorite pair of khakis isn't ruined! Just rub liquid laundry detergent into the stain with a brush as soon as possible. Or toss the garment into an oxygen-based stain remover and soak before you wash it. Of course, if the fabric's not machine washable, get thee to a dry-cleaner ASAP! Another tip our editor swears by is spraying hairspray onto the stain. Let it dry. Brush off the stain and launder as soon as possible.

chipmunk—about a tablespoon or two. Let the wine pool under your tongue, purse your lips, drop your chin, and breathe in. This aerates the wine while preventing the conspicuous slurp. And there is little to no chance of screwing this up so that the wine dribbles out of your mouth, down your chin, and onto the shirt you just spent your lunch money on dry-cleaning.

Good job! Okay, roll the wine over your tongue and gently swirl it around in your mouth. You'll notice that you taste sweetness (or notice the lack thereof) first. That's because the tip of your tongue is hardwired to recognize sweetness, while the sides of your tongue are programmed to register acidity. Among other reasons, acidity is important because it makes the wine taste refreshing—like lemons and limes, which also have high acidity. A wine is called

Wine-Tasting Maquillage

When you're going to a wine tasting—or anytime you know you'll be drinking especially good wine—lay off the heavy lipstick or lip gloss! Otherwise, you'll taste Luscious Cherry Shine instead of hints of black pepper in that glass of Shiraz. So go nude for a night, or apply just a light sheen of flavorless lip balm. Also, skip the sultry perfume—or dab on just the tiniest bit. Your senses of smell and taste are inextricably linked, so if you spray on loads of scent, you could throw off your ability to *taste* the wine as well. Wearing heavy scent at a wine tasting is considered *tres* gauche by oenophiles (that is, die-hard lovers of *vino*), so practice good etiquette.

"dry" if it doesn't have a lot of sugar in it, and "sweet" if it does. Pretty simple. But here's something to remember: Almost all table wines are technically called dry, even if some are less dry than others. Would you really want to pair something supersweet with that rack of lamb or with your plate of pasta primavera? No. It just wouldn't taste good. So when you're at a wine shop or restaurant, never say, "I'd like something dry," because that's the equivalent of walking into a shoe store and saying, "I'd like something with heels." The only wines that should really be sweet are dessert wines.

Later on in this chapter, we'll give you an easy-to-remember formula that'll help you choose the right wine—every time.

Then there's the alcohol. Without it, wine would feel as flat and boring as grape juice in your mouth. But there can be too much of a good thing. Most table wines are be between 9 percent and 14 percent alcohol. If there's too much alcohol, you'll know because you'll feel a "burn" at the back of your throat (and sometimes you can even smell it when you sniff the wine).

Lastly, if you're drinking red wine, you'll taste (and feel) the tannins in your mouth. Tannins are naturally occurring substances in red grape skins (and stems and seeds) that make your mouth feel dry, sort of like black tea or spinach does (although thanks to Candela Prol, New York City wine consultant, we can say with authority that the dryness spinach leaves in your mouth and on your teeth and gums feels like tannin, but isn't actually caused by it). Tannins add complexity to a wine.

Setting Up Your Home Wine Bar

Another excuse to go shopping! (Not that you need one, of course.) To enjoy wine—and to be able to serve it at the fabulous parties you're going to throw after you're done reading this book—you need a few basic items that you can store quite easily and compactly inside cabinets and drawers, no matter how small your house or apartment. (Megan should know because she lives in a shoebox-sized apartment up five flights of stairs in Manhattan.) And all the items you need can be purchased at just about any decent housewares store.

Don't think of this shopping trip as just another errand, like buying a coat rack or garbage bags. You're about to set up your Very Own Wine Bar. If you're like us, you've always dreamed of owning a bar—haven't you? (You haven't? Maybe it's just us. Still, setting up shop is lots of fun!)

Wineglasses

Although it is common to see different types of glassware for red and white wine, it is not necessary. A good all-purpose wineglass must have a generous bowl that tapers toward the mouth in order to focus the bouquet while allowing enough room for swirling without spilling. You can get perfectly decent glasses for about $5 to $10 a pop. No need to spend more—unless someone's buying them for you!

In victory, you deserve Champagne; in defeat, you need it.
—Napoleon Bonaparte

When it comes to Champagne glasses, let's clear something up here. Those wide-mouthed glasses—which, legend has it, were molded after Marie Antoinette's breasts—are good for nothing. (As were Marie and her breasts, after that "Let them eat cake" comment.) Not only do they make it supremely easy to slosh the bubbly all over your new Betsey Johnson skirt, but they also wreck what is arguably one of the greatest beverages in the world. Their superwide mouths increase the surface of the Champagne that's exposed to air, killing the effervescence and making the stuff as flat as a pancake. It's the equivalent of spending two hours donning your best black pants, heels, and slinky top, blowing your hair dry, and turning lipstick application into an art—and then standing under the shower for fifteen minutes. The lesson? Get Champagne flutes, those tall, skinny glasses.

Corkscrew

Not nearly as complex as you might believe. Buy one, and use it. Do not be afraid of it. You're stronger than it is. Get the kind with the arms that rise as you twist downward. Our friend Aileen, an Irish woman who knows a remarkable amount about wine, imbibing in general, and removing any obstacles between herself and a drink, calls this type of corkscrew a "Jumpin' Jimmy O'Reilly." To see why, hold the circular bottom of a corkscrew in your left hand, and with your right hand, pull the handle up and down. The arms, too, will fly up and down, making the corkscrew look like a stick figure doing jumping jacks. Isn't it wonderful to be easily amused? Anyway, it costs about $5, is nearly impossible to break, and can be found just about everywhere including housewares stores, supermarkets, liquor stores, etc. Some experts denounce Jumpin' Jimmy O'Reilly, because he's not 100 percent foolproof, and if he's not used properly, you might get some cork in your wine. We say, what's the point? It's the most common type of cork-screw, so why not just take the path of least resistance and learn how to use the damn thing? Once you do, it's really a no-brainer.

You really don't need to get the Swiss Army–style, manpowered corkscrew that waiters tote around (unless you're a waiter). It takes some practice to master, and it's a bigger hassle than returning a sweater at the Gap the day after Christmas.

Foil Cutter

Our favorite style is a little plastic circular device with a metal blade inside. Its fits over the top of an unopened bottle of wine to remove the foil covering. It costs about $5 to $8, takes up no space at all, and is highly preferable to breaking a fingernail or four trying to peel the foil off by hand. It's often part of a set of wine-opening tools, but see if you can find one loose.

Wine Cooler

No, not the piña colada– and strawberry daiquiri–flavored horrors you drank in college. This kind of wine cooler is a newer, sleeker alternative to the traditional ice bucket. Many of them are made of stainless steel with a plastic interior, and they insulate your bottle of white wine. This way, the wine stays cold during that romantic tête-a-tête, so you don't have to keep running to the fridge or lift a dripping bottle from a bucket. Plus, ice buckets actually tend to keep the wine around the temperature of a Sno-Cone, while white wine should really be kept at around 50 degrees. Look for the style of wine cooler that fits both a Champagne and a table-wine bottle.

Label Remover

Finally! An answer to the other unpeelable thing on a wine bottle—the label. You can buy a packet of label removers for about $9 at a good-size housewares store or liquor store. What you get is a packet of clear plastic film coated with strong adhesive that, when applied to the wine label, splits it and removes only the printed surface, leaving you with a label attached to a clear plastic patch. Now, when you're enjoying a bottle you wish could be bottomless, you can easily lift off the label and take it with you as a reminder of exactly which wine rang your bell. And if you want to find it again, you can take the label to your local wine shop or liquor store and match the labels. Or, if you're scrapbook happy, you can even paste your favorite labels into a notebook so you can reference them later.

Wine Charms and Bottler Stoppers

We usually like to keep a couple other accoutrements lying around, like those cute little wineglass charms you might have seen at gift stores. They're used for identifying whose glass is whose. While charms aren't for every occasion, they're fun to use if you're having, say, a girls' night in with a few friends and a few more bottles of your vino of choice. That way you won't be holding your glasses up to the light and trying to decipher lipstick stains to figure out whose glass belongs to whom.

Be sure to invest in a couple of wine bottle stoppers. If you're like us, you inevitably misplace, toss, or somehow break the cork the second you get the damn thing out of the bottle. Stoppers go for about $2.50 a pop, which is a small price to pay for convenience and decent preservation of the wine in question—and you won't get little crumbs of cork in the bottle from trying to jam the cork back in. Although many wine snobs would be appalled, we use 'em for sparkling wines, too. After all, are you really going to let Champagne sit around the fridge for a few days? No, my friend, you are not! You're going to drink the leftovers with brunch on Sunday morning.

Notebook

Trust us, you will *not* remember the name of that stellar Riesling you found at a restaurant or tasted at a wine shop. Not writing down the name of a fabulous wine you encounter is like trying on the perfect pair of black pants at a sample sale—then not buying them. You might be able to find the pants again tomorrow, or at another store; but there's a good chance they may be lost forever. Don't let this happen to you! Get a notebook. It doesn't have to cost a lot, and it can be anything from one of those marble composition notebooks to a pocket-size journal. Of course, if you plan to paste labels in it, you'll want to make sure your notebook is large enough to accommodate them. Megan carries a tiny hardcover journal in her bag; it's sturdy enough not to get damaged, but small enough so it doesn't add a lot of extra bulk. That way, she's always prepared.

Extra Credit: A Handy Six-Bottle Wine Rack

There's no need to spend a lot of money on a small wine rack, so skip the wine connoisseur's catalog and the pricey department stores, and head for a discount department store. There you'll be able to find quite a nice little number to the tune of $15. Why do you need a wine rack? Because it stores bottles horizontally, so you don't have to worry about them rolling off shelves or tables and breaking. (Not only would that be a royal pain to clean up, it'd be a waste of money.) Most important, storing bottles on their sides keeps the corks moistened with wine, so there's less chance of the cork drying out and cracking or letting in oxygen and ruining the wine. And, of course, wine racks just look cool.

Given that space is at a premium in city apartments, you may be tempted to fit your wine rack on top of the fridge or a cabinet so you don't have to waste precious counterspace. Don't do it. In general, it's not a good idea to store bottles of wine high up in a room that's not climate controlled, where temperature fluctuations are more extreme. Place your wine rack at counter level and away from any sources of extreme heat or cold, such as the radiator, stove, or air conditioner.

Storing Wine

Speaking of looking cool, a quick word to the wise about storing your unopened bottles of wine. Keep them in a cool place with low light. Too much heat and light can absolutely screw up wine, so don't store the bottles near a window or a radiator. Then again, don't put them out on your windowsill during a December snowstorm, either. Around 70 degrees—year-round—is fine for most wines.

Storing wine is like storing shoes. You've got your Nikes, your knee-high boots, your four-inch pink stilettos that you can't believe you nabbed for 50 percent off, and the heels that look great with every suit you've got. Now, if you take them off carefully, arrange them on a shoe rack, and keep them in their boxes when they're out of season, your shoes will serve you faithfully and well. But if you continuously stumble home in a drunken stupor, rip them off your feet after limping twenty blocks in them, and fling them under the futon or trample them when you get dressed the next morning, they'll commit treason and fall apart.

Same with wine. Treat your wine well, even if you're planning on drinking all the bottles relatively soon. After

Dress Up That Glass of Vino!

Put frozen grapes into white wine. Frozen grapes are better than ice cubes because grapes won't melt and water down the wine. And anyway, you shouldn't put ice cubes in white wine at all, because it should already be chilled! However, there are some people who, in the comfort of their own home, insist on doing it. Frozen grapes are a good alternative for folks who think they *need* ice cubes in wine!

all, what fun is a dinner party or a wine-and-cheese affair if, after you open that Pinot Noir, your guests ask for Diet Coke?

We always keep white wines in the fridge; as soon as we bring 'em home, we pop 'em in there so that we'll never be stuck saying, "Dang, Mr. Hot Date Whom I've Brought Home For A Drink, I've got the most amazing bottle of Portuguese Vinho Verde, but I'm afraid I can't offer you a glass because the stuff isn't chilled." But know that refrigeration is really suitable only for white wines you're going to drink within the next month or two.

Since you're the Diva of Drinks, the Bombshell of Bartending, you probably have the basic bar booze on hand—vodka, rum, gin, perhaps some tequila or scotch. Good woman!

The next time you're at the liquor store, invest in a couple of extras, like a small bottle of bitters and a bottle of (inexpensive) crème de cassis. Bitters and a sugar cube turn Champagne or sparkling wine into a Champagne cocktail, and crème de cassis concocts the classic Kir Royale. You know that accessories can make or break an outfit, and that a couple of well-placed pieces can transform "blah" into "bang." Similarly, these drinkable accessories are great to have in your arsenal to spice up an average sparkling wine—as well as take the edge off a less than stellar bottle of vino. Especially for parties, when your buddy shows up with a bargain-basement sparkler. "Oh Janet, how sweet! You shouldn't have. I mean, you *really* shouldn't have. You know, I just happen to have some cassis right here; Kirs for everyone!"

Popping and Pouring?

Girls, your days of struggling with wine bottles, or—gasp!—leaving their opening to the men, are over. No more! You are now an enlightened, wine-savvy woman who is quite capable, thank you, of cracking open your own bottle of vino, and serving it up with ease and élan.

Earlier, we were rambling on about how easy it is to use the wing-style corkscrew (or, rather, Jumpin' Jimmy). And we weren't giving you a crock. Here's a (relatively) foolproof method for opening a bottle of wine gracefully with this type of corkscrew.

With your nondominant hand (Would that be your submissive hand? Ooh, kinky!), grab the bottle by the neck. If it's chilled, use a towel so your hand doesn't slip on the condensation. Let the wings of the corkscrew relax, so that Jimmy's arms are at his sides. Now, with your dominant hand, place the tip of the corkscrew in the very center of the cork. (Center it as accurately as you can, and you'll have less chance of breaking the cork.) Curve the

If you're having that incredibly hot guy who works down the hall over for wine, and a bit of cork manages to find its way into the bottle and then his glass, never fear; all is not lost. If he's in another room, just scoop it out with a teaspoon. He'll never even know. If he's right next to you, say something clever like, "Ooh, you got the lucky piece of cork! That means you win a prize—which I'll give you later." *Then* scoop it out with a spoon. Cork doesn't ruin a wine or even change its flavor; it's harmless. So don't sweat it!

thumb and forefinger of your other hand around the circular part of the corkscrew (as if you were making a dorky "okay" hand signal), and hold onto the bottle's neck with your other fingers. With your dominant hand on the key-shaped handle, *push straight down and twist* with a clockwise motion. Keep going until the wings are all the way up, or till you can't see the screw part of the corkscrew anymore. Then just push the wings down with both hands, and the cork should slide out neatly. Untwist it from the corkscrew, have a look at it just for fun, and toss it. (You're going to be using your brand-new wine stopper to keep it fresh, remember?)

If it takes you a couple of tries to master the ol' corkscrew, don't stress. It's just a matter of practice, so don't be intimidated. And the great thing is, the more you "practice," the more wine you get to drink!

Manual Corkscrew

Just in case you ever encounter this beast, it's just the screwy part of the corkscrew attached to some kind of handle, usually either plastic, metal, or wood. Pretty simple. Just like you did with the winged corkscrew, place the sharp tip smack in the middle of the cork. Then push straight down and twist clockwise; with this type of corkscrew, it's as important to push straight down as it is to get to the Barney's warehouse sale early.

If the corkscrew beats a crooked path through the cork, the cork will be a mangled mess. (If you show up at the Barney's sale late, *you'll* be a mangled mess.) So show it who's boss.

Pouring Wine

The waiters in that five-star restaurant really look like they know what they're doing when they pour wine, don't they? That's because they do. When you pour wine, your goal is to get it into the glass relatively quickly, efficiently, and without spilling. Hold the bottle in your dominant hand, and the glass in your other hand (or set the glass on a flat surface, slide the stem of the glass between the index and middle fingers of your other hand, and press down on the base gently to keep it steady). Lift the bottle so it's at about a 90-degree angle with the glass, then tilt it and pour at a controlled speed for about five seconds (Megan counts in her head: one-stop, two-stop, three-stop, four-stop, five-stop. Hey, it's cheesy, but it works). The amount of time to pour may vary depending on the size of the glassware. Be mindful to leave enough room to comfortably swirl the wine, never filling past the halfway point. And here's the part where you'll look cool: Right after "five-stop," snap the bottle up and give it a little twist inward with your wrist. (Ever cradle the ball in high school lacrosse? Sort of a similar motion.) Give it a couple practice tries, but once you get it down, you won't spill a drop, and you'll look superprofessional.

Pouring Sparkling Wine

When Megan was a kid, her dad taught her an important life lesson. "You know, Megan," he said, "Some things in life are all froth, and no Guinness." Don't let your bottle of sparkling wine be one of them! All that foam is fun, but

So you're at a chichi restaurant with your boss and the most important clients ever. Everyone's ordering a glass of wine before dinner—and you have no idea what to get. Your brain is so addled you've forgotten everything you've learned in this book. What to do? Just order a glass of the least expensive sparkling wine. You'll look festive and knowledgeable, and it's a refreshing way to cleanse your palate before dinner. Plus, it goes with just about everything. A no-brainer!

heck, you paid good money for the stuff, so why let any of it overflow? Plus, the more bubbles that pour out of the bottle, the fewer bubbles remain in the sparkling wine. And correct us if we're wrong, but we suspect you want your sparking wine to remain sparkling for as long as possible. How to foil the fizz? Hold the glass near the top of the stem (when you're pouring any white wine, you should hold the stem only, so you don't warm up the vino prematurely), and before you pour, tilt the glass slightly, at about a 30- to 45-degree angle. This prevents overfoaming and overflowing. Your guests—and their clothes—will thank you!

Pouring It Out:
How Long Should You Keep Wine?

So you're straightening up after that little wine-and-cheese soiree, you've got a half-drunk bottle of Cabernet and an almost-full bottle of Pinot Grigio on your hands. What to do? Well, first of all, don't throw the stuff out. Wine can keep for a few days in the fridge, so pop a stopper in each, and stick them in with the leftovers. (If at all possible, try not to store superpungent leftovers—especially garlicky ones—near the wine. Although the stoppers will protect it from most scents, treating your opened wines to a nonstinky fridge can't do any harm and may do some good.) Both red and white wines can be kept cold after opening; but before you drink the red, let it warm up to room temperature (or about 65 degrees Fahrenheit). How long can you keep opened wines? Here's a handy little chronology to follow:

Day One: Not as good as the day before, usually, but most wines will still be eminently drinkable. Still okay to serve to guests—but make sure you taste it first, just in case.

Day Two: Going downhill quicker than Ben and J.Lo's engagement. Just polish the thing off, for the love of Pete! Get someone to come over and help with it, if need be.

Day Three: If anyone's drinking it at this point, it should be you and only you. Or someone you really don't like.

What about keeping sparkling wine or Champagne fresh? Ah, if only we could inject it with a magical Fountain of Youth serum! Alas—and we're being realists, not pessimists—sparklers are dying from the minute you open them. Those tiny, fragile bubbles fly up to the surface of the wine as soon as it's exposed to air, and the more time it's exposed to air, the flatter the stuff becomes. Thus, you really should drink the entire bottle of a sparkling wine. (Yes, we know it's a chore.) If, for some reason unknown to us, you should have some left over, seal it with a wine stopper and drink it the next morning with brunch. Feel free to doctor it up with orange, cranberry, or pineapple juice.

Let Your Sommelier Be Your Guide: Navigating Restaurant Wine Lists

Many a savvy Downtown Girl has been stumped when faced with a wine list in an "I'm too sexy for *you*" restaurant of the moment. Combine a wine list the length of a Ph.D. dissertation with the pain of a push-up bra and strappy stilettos—in February—and it's no wonder many women defer to their dinner companions to make the wine selection. Don't be intimidated! Wine lists are easier to decode than you think, we promise! Your wine list will probably be broken down in a couple different ways. First, it'll be divided into wines by the glass and wines by the bottle, then by red wines, whites, and sparklers. Each entry will look something like this:

Chateau Buckley, Pinot Noir, New York, N.Y., 2002

This is a Pinot Noir produced by Chateau Buckley, located in New York, N.Y., and the grapes were harvested in 2002. Not so hard, right?

Your best resource in a wine-y establishment is your server or the sommelier (the wine steward). But first, let's get rid of the idea that these people are the experts and you're the idiot. Mais non. Think of the server as your tour guide. It is not the server's job to make you feel dumb or to sell you an expensive bottle of wine you don't want. And the vast majority of servers would never try to do that. So it's in your best interest to trust them. But, as in any successful relationship, communication is key. To get what you want, you have to tell them what you want. But what *do* you want? Think about these three questions:

1. How much do you want to spend?
2. What do you want your wine to taste like?
3. What are you going to eat with it (if anything)?

One good way to give your wine selection a little direction is to order something to eat. That way your server or sommelier will have something to pair the wine with and there's a much greater chance that you'll get what you want. Look your server soulfully in the eye and use this magic formula:

I'm looking to spend ___ on something that tastes like ___ and that matches well with _____.

We know you're no shrinking violet, so go ahead and have a conversation with him or her about what you want. That's part of a server's job. Usually he or she will help direct you from there.

Eau de Attitude

By and large, most servers and sommeliers will be gracious and accommodating. However, sometimes you'll get stuck with one who, out of ignorance or pretension, just isn't interested in helping you choose a wine. This is a sad thing. Let's have a moment of silence to reflect on just how sad it is.

Okay. Time's up. It's so sad because you can learn so much from a helpful, knowledgeable sommelier or server. They, your tour guides, can skillfully lead you through the vast world of wine; or they can leave you stranded on a dead-end street with a tourists' map in your hand and a bunch of thugs approaching you. Get the picture? Good. If you find yourself in this situation, here are a few tips for finding your way into the good part of town, so to speak.

If you can, always buy wine by the bottle instead of the glass at a restaurant or bar. (Of course, this rule doesn't apply if you find yourself alone, or are just meeting a friend or colleague for a quick drink.) A bottle of wine is almost always a better investment than a glass. The bottle won't have been previously opened, so there's no chance of being stuck with a glass of something that's been sitting around for a few days.

. . . .

Hangover Cure #143

Eat salt. (We are especially pleased to be able to advise this, because we're the kind of girls who dip each individual French fry in a big pile of salt on the side of our plates.) Eating salt will encourage you to drink water, and because salt causes you to retain water, it'll prevent you from becoming more dehydrated than you already are. Megan prefers a combination of salt and grease. Try corn chips, pretzels with a chunk of cheese on the side, or, if you're feeling brunch-y, bacon and eggs with a liberal dose of salt and pepper.

First—and this goes for wines by the glass and by the bottle—write off the top two most expensive wines on the list (unless you've already tried it and know that you love it). Why? Well, why spend a lot on something you're not sure you'll even like? The exception to this: Some bars and restaurants will give you a splash of wine to taste before you buy a glass. Next, write off the cheapest two wines. The cheapest ones are probably priced to move quickly. Go for something midrange. When in complete doubt, we say go with something you've never heard of but that appeals to you. This is part of the whole spirit of enjoying wine— being adventurous and trying new things! After all, it's just a glass of wine, not a BMW. If it's something you don't like, just "chalk it up to education," as Megan's father would say, and move on—preferably to a less pretentious and more accommodating restaurant or wine bar!

Good Vino Loves Company: How to Order Wine for the Table

If it hasn't happened already, you might find yourself at dinner with friends, clients, or (God forbid) your in-laws, and for whatever reason (it's your corporate card, you're taking his mom out for her birthday . . .), choosing the wine becomes your call. First of all, don't panic. You're not going to screw up. Don't just yell "Chardonnay!" and hide under the table.

Now, we can't possibly predict the wine lists—or the menus—for every restaurant you'll ever encounter, so here

Restaurant Etiquette

Sniffing the cork makes you look stupid. Don't do it. After the waiter opens your bottle of wine, he may indeed hand you the cork (or set it down on the table next to your glass). It's imprinted with the name of the winery and the wine. Why? Once upon a time, shady winemakers often tried to scam their customers by pilfering corks from better wines and sticking them into bottles of—the equivalent of what you find in the bottom of the bargain barrel at your local liquor store!

are a couple of tips to keep in mind when the choice of wine falls to you. (We'll elaborate a bit on food and wine pairing in the following chapters.)

First, ask everyone what they are thinking of eating. If you're enjoying food and wine together, you absolutely *must* choose the food first. (We don't understand why servers often ask if you know what sort of wine you'd like *before* you've even had a chance to glance at the menu.) Then ask if anyone has any preferences. If Mrs. In-Law hates Cabernet Sauvignon, why subject her to it against her will?

Now, take a look at the wine list. You'll want to order one bottle for every four to six people. Since you're trying to make a good impression here, if you see a wine that you've already had, even if it's something on the pricey side, by all means order it (as long as it matches decently with everyone's food). That gets rid of 99.9 percent of the guesswork. Basically, you're all set! If nothing on the list is familiar to you, though, you'll have to do a little sleuthing.

NEW YORK CITY

Grapes in the Big Apple! **New York City**'s abundance of great bars and restaurants—many with drop-dead gorgeous wine lists—make the city an excellent place to sample any and every kind of wine.

Visit **Punch and Judy** (26 Clinton St., Manhattan, ☎212-982-1116), a hip-but-never-snooty wine bar where the young, knowledgeable staff is eager to tell you about the latest wine trends and answer all your questions.

Head out to Brooklyn and order up a glass at **DOC** (83 N. 7th St., Brooklyn, ☎718-963-1925), a cozy, laid-back joint featuring simple, delicious food and equally great wines.

If you're feeling more upscale, head to the downtown branch of the famous **Morrell's** (900 Broadway, Manhattan, ☎212-253-0900), a bit more hip and laid-back than its uptown cousin. Here the world of wine is laid out before you.

Remember, don't let anyone—waiter, rude dinner guest, whomever—push you into spending any more than you want to. *You're* buying; it's *your* call. Of course you don't want to look cheap, but you don't need to order that wildly expensive Merlot. Look for something midpriced, between $25 and $50. We don't think you ever need to spend more than $50 for a good bottle of wine at a restaurant.

Red or white? The ultimate conundrum. Traditionally, white wines go with white meat and red wines go with red meat. To that sentence we add, "sometimes." Some lighter reds can be just ducky with char-grilled chicken, for example, or oilier fish like salmon and tuna, or lean pork. Also, there are a handful of whites that can be served with red meat. Fuller bodied, off-dry whites such as Riesling, Gewürztraminer, and Sémillon pair nicely with rich and spicy meals such as BBQ, lamb kebabs, and Latin dishes. Be judicious, however, because heavy red meat will overpower even the very best whites. If everyone's eyeing chicken or fish, order white. If they're gazing longingly at beef, game, or heavy pork entrées in the same way you stare at the window of a Prada store, make it red. If the table's split, go for a light red, like Pinot Noir, or a Beaujolais. This won't work if half your group is noshing on delicate white fish like cod, so keep your fingers crossed and recommend the tuna.

Now that you've got a firm idea of price in mind, summon your server. You've got a 90 percent chance that he or she will be relatively knowledgeable about the wine list—a high enough percentage to gamble on. Tell your server what you want in as much detail as humanly possible, with that magic formula. For example, "I'm looking to spend around $30 to $35 on a red wine that's spicy and peppery, and will stand up to red sauce." Your server (and especially your sommelier, if you're lucky enough to be eating at a place that has one) will be able to make some informed recommendations. Plus, if you've got more than six people in your party, you're in luck; you'll definitely need two bottles, anyway, since one bottle equals six glasses at the most. Hallelujah! Order one red and one white.

While we swear by the magic formula, sometimes mentioning price is inappropriate (business dinners and first dates, for example). What to do? Simply omit the first part of the magic formula and say, "I'm looking for something that tastes like _____ and that matches well with _____." A good server will give you options in a variety of price ranges. However, if the server insists on steering you only toward bottles of wine that cost more than your car payment, simply bat your eyelashes and say, "Those look wonderful and, tell me, what would you recommend for a *midrange* Merlot?" (or Chardonnay or Pinot Noir . . .) He'll get the point.

If worse comes to worse and you're totally stuck about what to order, take heart! If you're looking for reds, no one hates a nice big fruity Zinfandel (the red kind, not the kind with the misnomer "white"!) from the United States or Australia. Desperately seeking a white? It's very, very hard to get something crappy from Germany or Austria. Skip the Chardonnay if you're stumped; we know it's a name you probably recognize and that recognition may be as comfortable as your favorite jeans, but cheap Chardonnays abound and you're likely to encounter a bad one.

Looking for the fruit of the vine in **San Francisco?** You'll find it at the **PlumpJack Wine Store** (3201 Fillmore St. ☎888 415-9463). Owned by the city's current mayor, this store boasts a staggering selection of over 500 wines. If you're not sure what you're looking for, just ask the well-informed staff. Oh, and the store doesn't carry anything the staff doesn't like, so you can rest assured that the staff has sampled everything they're selling!

Now, since you're running the show here, when the server returns to your table with the wine, he or she will pour a splash into your glass. This is for you to taste and approve. Swirl it around, give it a quick sniff, and then taste it; then, if you find it to your liking, Your Highness, nod at the waiter and say something like, "That's fine, thanks." Then your server will fill everyone's glasses and will place the wine back on the table. (If the server walks away with the wine, don't jump up and run after him or her. Since the server is often in charge of filling guests' glasses, sometimes the server will just get it out of your way. But don't be shy about taking charge; if you'd rather pour the wine for the table, just tell the server.)

Remember, getting a "bad" bottle of wine is pretty rare, and when you're faced with one, you'll usually know without a doubt. It'll smell awful and will actually get worse the longer it sits out. Try not to confuse "bad" with "something I've never had before." If you're trying a new kind of wine, and you're not thrilled with your first sip or two, give it a chance. Sometimes it'll grow on you after a little while. Or, you might want to order something to eat; food can make even the lowest-quality wine taste like ambrosia. Immediately nibble something with a little fat and protein; chances are, you'll notice a big difference.

Eight Egregious Wine Myths—Debunked!

Think the conventional wine wisdom is foolproof? Think again! Before we send you off into the world of wine

Downtown style, we'd like to explode a few vinous myths, from believing everything you read to drinking white wine in summer only. Then you'll be ready to hit the world of red wine, white wine, sparkling wine—and beyond!

1. **The critics are always right.** No way! Wine experts and critics are people, too, and their (very informed) opinions can differ drastically. So there's no such thing as "right" and "wrong." Most wine experts—and wine lovers—encourage novice imbibers to trust their own palates; it makes the world of wine much less confusing.

2. **Wine is hard to understand, and only connoisseurs who use brain-bogglingly big words can enjoy it.** Not so! "Be honest—don't worry about the jargon," says Tim McDonnell, bartender at East of Eighth, a laid-back, crowded haunt in New York City's super-hip Chelsea neighborhood. Throwing around strange terms you don't know the first thing about usually guarantees an embarrassing situation (and one that does not usually translate into a good joke to tell your friends). "Don't pretend," Tim urges. "Say what you feel!" Amen, Tim. If you think your glass of Pinot Noir smells like a barnyard or the chocolate-covered cherries your grandfather used to give you, then that's what it smells like. Period.

3. **You can drink white wine only in summer.** Why, because it's served cold? Does that mean you wouldn't drink a beer or a mixed drink over ice in January, either? While cool white wine can be very refreshing

in the summer months, weather shouldn't dictate your choice of wine. Your taste in wine—and what food you're pairing it with—should!

4. **Sparkling wine is for New Year's and mimosas are for bridal showers. Period.** We're ashamed to say that we operated under this myth for a very long time. Then one fateful evening, at a wine bar with friends, we said what the hell, and ordered a glass of Prosecco, a light, sparkling wine from the Veneto region of Italy. Super-refreshing, it perked us right up—and it was the perfect match for the fried calamari we were noshing. It's an excellent palate cleanser, with lots of reasonable selections on many wine lists and in stores. Besides, every day's a celebration!

5. **Good wine is always old wine**. ("But I just bought a bottle of German Riesling. I don't want to wait years before I can drink it; I'm thirsty now!"). This one elicits a collective "Argh!" from wine educator Gwendolyn Wilson and wine consultant Lori Schimmel, both in New York City. While many wines do improve with age, not all of them do. The vast majority of (very good!) wines produced are made to be drunk within a year. So unless your wine rack is full of $100-plus bottles you've purchased after doing extensive research, time's a-wasting. Drink 'em now.

6. **If I ask the server, sommelier, or liquor store owner for "a nice dry wine," I'll get just what I'm looking for**. Whoa there, Missy (with apologies to our very wine-savvy friend, Missy). Tell someone you want a dry wine, and all that says is, "Sir, I do not want

Manischewitz or communion wine tonight." Well, that's generally a given (unless, of course, it's Passover or if you're at church). Instead, be as specific as possible—the more detail, the better. Something like, "I'm looking for a red wine in the $15 range that's peppery, spicy, and goes well with salmon" will usually get you what you're looking for.

7. **Synthetic corks are cheesy! Plus, they don't keep wine as well as their natural counterparts.** Gwendolyn Wilson, says, "Absolutely not!" The fact is, corks are fallible. They're porous. They're made from trees. They can occasionally go bad. Screw tops can't. So don't judge a wine by its cover! More and more winemakers—including some of the best in the business—are choosing screw caps over corks these days.

8. **Good wine is too expensive. I'd rather spend the money on a new pair of knee-high boots!** Well, we're pleased to tell you that you can have your boots and eat them, too. Or something like that. Let's put it this way: many expensive wines taste quite good; but you'd be surprised at the vast number of interesting, drinkable, pairable-with-food wines that are relatively inexpensive (for these purposes, we'll define "relatively inexpensive" as $20 or less). Don't believe us? Check out a wine magazine, and you'll see that the critics agree. Many magazines rate wines in the back of the magazine and you'll see that $15 bottles and $70 bottles often receive the same score in their blind tastings. (Of course, now you know that wine is so much more than just a number—but you get our drift!) Besides, notes

Lee Fleming, sommelier at Tse Yang, a fine Manhattan restaurant, historically, wine isn't a rich girl's libation. In fact, throughout most of history, it was made by peasant farmers.

The Veritas of Vino

Well, ladies, you've now been formally introduced to that crazy little thing called wine. You know how it's made, why red wine is red and white wine is, well, yellow. Ordering a bottle of wine at a chichi restaurant? Not a problem. Would you ever, ever, in your wildest dreams, even consider sniffing the cork? *No!* Now that we've painted the broad strokes, read on for the finer points about vino. But believe us, the games are just beginning. Keep reading to find out which wines are hot now, how to throw a wine-and-cheese soiree with panache, how to seduce a man with wine, and tons more. But first, let's toast—to you!

Chapter Two

The World of White Wine

Ladies, you know it's perfectly acceptable to drink red or white wine any time of year. But there's nothing that can replace a cool glass of white wine on a warm evening or a sultry Saturday when all you want to do is lie outside, work on your tan, and skim the newspaper or the latest edition of your favorite magazine. What do we love about white wines? Well, they're certainly no less complex than their red counterparts that are full of earthy, animally, red-fruit scents and flavors. Whites are packed with the taste and smell of yummy yellowish orange fruit such as peaches, apricots, oranges, and grapefruits; flowers such as roses and violets; herbs and vegetables such as freshly cut grass and green and white pepper. (Although no single wine sports all of these, of course!)

In this chapter, we'll take no prisoners. Guerrilla-style, we're going to debunk myths like "Only red wine can be paired with cheese," "Never drink white wine with red meat—ever!" and—drumroll, please—we'll tell you why Chardonnay is *so* not the last word in white wine. And because there's lots happening around the world when it comes to whites, we give you the scoop on the hottest Italian whites, and why it's next to impossible to screw up with German whites, even if you've got no idea how to pronounce "gesundheit." Plus we spill the beans about some super-refreshing whites from Greece.

We hope you're ready for a good time, because we teach you some tricks of the trade for throwing a wine-and-cheese party with verve and style, where the hottest wine bars are in your city, the best white wines for just $10 or less, and lots more. Oh, and no more scratching your head while staring blankly at your closet—we've even got some inspired ideas for what to wear while you're sipping your vino of choice. So break out the corkscrew, grab a glass, slip into something more comfortable—and let the imbibing begin!

Chardonnay: White Burgundy

There's no question about it: Chardonnay (shar-dun-NAY) is the most popular wine in the country. Whether it's from France, Chile, Australia, California, or Washington State, it's being sucked up by thirsty Americans faster than you can say "oak-aged wine spritzer." Of course, our motto is drink what you like, but we think that a lot of Americans choose Chardonnay by default. And we're here to change that, ladies! There's so much Chardonnay produced today that it's not always easy to find a good one. One example of a "bad" Chardonnay is the superoaky kind. It's been aged in oak barrels (or had oak extract added to it) and taste like a mouthful of vanilla-tinged wood. In our opinion, why cover up a grape's personality with oak? (The Chardonnay grape is often described as "versatile." Could that be synonymous for "no personality at all"? Perhaps.)

Then again, Megan's disdain for Chardonnay could stem from her painful childhood, in which her mother always drank cheap, boxed Chardonnay with dinner. To be sure, when Megan turned twenty-one, she drank it herself (that and quite a few other things). But still she wondered, where's the verve, style, and freshness of the wines she had in, say, Germany, as a "young but legal to drink in Europe" lass? Those qualities certainly couldn't be found in that cardboard box in the fridge. Somewhere deep in the hills of France well-made Chardonnays do exist. So you'll have to decide for yourself: Is the most popular wine in the United States dramatically overrated, or does it live up to its reputation?

You can grow Chardonnay grapes just about anywhere there's dirt. (Under your bed? Maybe.) Chardonnay's Mecca has always been the Burgundy region of France, where wines made from Chardonnay are known as white burgundies, and where winemakers have been creating some of the best—and often only *subtlety* oaky—representations of the stuff for centuries. It's not always easy to find a reasonably priced white Burgundy. Then there's the Chablis region, where Chardonnay-based wines are often unoaked—sometimes resulting in quite nice, dry, minerally wines. (Remember those characterless jugs of Chablis your parents used to buy and pour over ice cubes? Yep. Those are also made from the Chardonnay grape.)

In the New World—basically, anywhere outside of France—Chardonnays tend to have that buttery, woodsy, vanilla-tinged taste and scent that comes from oaking. You'll find some, though, that are fruity, with scents and flavors of apple and pear among others, and sometimes even ones that are spicy and smoky. California produces many good Chardonnays with these rich characteristics. In Australia, peaches, melons, and tropical fruits are the signature tastes and scents. Chile's Chardonnays are still emerging, and although a lot are just oaked within an inch of their lives, some do sport fresh-fruit flavors and interesting spiciness.

What to eat with Chardonnay? Ah, there's the question. Some experts say Chardonnay goes with everything—some say it goes with nothing. We say, look, if you really love a glass of Chard with that pepperoni pizza, go with God. But you can't go wrong pairing the stuff with fatty foods, especially anything with a lot of butter. Chardonnay's a great choice to bring to a clambake! If you're bored with that overly oaky taste of bad Chardonnay, then the next time you're at a very vino-friendly restaurant ask for a *smoky* Chardonnay. The taste of smoke in a white wine is especially intriguing—a nice change from all that straight sweetness!

Lastly ladies, we don't mean to "dis"—to borrow a gem of a word from the eighties—anyone who's an avid drinker of Chardonnay. Just know that a huge, practically boundless world of excellent white wines is out there—so please, don't limit yourself to what you know!

What is Chardonnay good for, beyond a doubt? (No, "getting drunk" is not the answer.) It's one of the principal grapes in Champagne!

If You Like Chardonnay

If you like Chardonnay try a Chardonnay/Sémillon blend from Washington State or Australia. The dose of Sémillon kicks Chardonnay up a notch!

What to Wear?

Oh, who cares? Wear whatever the hell you want. But seriously, folks, if you're drinking a fairly standard, oak-soaked Chard, feel free to keep it casual. Because it's a crowd pleaser (a fact we hate to face), bring a bottle to a poolside barbecue and sip a glass while bikini clad.

Sauvignon Blanc

Nope, it has nothing to do with Cabernet Sauvignon! (The Sauvignon Blanc grape, a white grape, could actually be the opposite of the Cabernet Sauvignon grape, a red grape.) Sauvignon Blanc's mother country is France, where you might see the wine labeled as Pouilly-Fumé or Sancerre, but today, Sauvignon Blanc flourishes around the world, in New Zealand, South Africa, and the good ol' United States (where it's often called Fumé Blanc). And prices range from around $7 to, well, a lot more than that. Lots of Sauvs smell like freshly cut grass, green bell peppers, herbs, gooseberries, or even—believe it or not—cat urine. Some versions are very, very dry and have mouth-puckering acidity, while others, especially versions from California that aren't oaky, have fruity characteristics, like apple, pear, or citrus. Believe us, they'll make you hungry! Try one with a first course, such as a simple salad, or any other kind of vegetable, for that matter. And its classic food partner is raw shellfish (superseductive in itself!).

Sauvignon Blanc is popular, has been popular for years, and probably ever shall be, world without end, Amen. It's grown in so many locales internationally, so where can you find a good one at a decent price? Start with New Zealand, which exports quite a few nice citrusy versions at around $13 a bottle. Serve Sauvignon Blanc with shrimp scampi on New Year's Eve, or raw clams at the beach in July. And if you're ordering American Sauvs in a restaurant, here's a tip: If the server or sommelier uses the words "vanilla," "woodsy," "creamy," or "oaky" when describing it, it's probably been aged in oak. And you know how we feel about oaky white wines—not good. Megan just had a California Sauvignon Blanc that tasted exactly like bad Chardonnay. No, thank you!

If You Like Sauvignon Blanc

If you're a Sauv drinker then chances are you're not looking for a whole lot of lush fruit. Try a tart Pinot Gris from Oregon, a superdry (or *sec*) Vouvray from France, another great seafood companion; or even an Italian Vermentino.

What to Wear?

Sharp, crisp Sauvignon Blanc calls for classic elegance. Balance a glass in one hand and a raw oyster in the other while you're clad in black, perhaps a knee-length tank dress or a hip-length top over sleek pants. Add simple silver hoops, and you're good to go from the office to the wine bar to dinner—where you'll be presiding over the wine selection, of course!

Pinot Gris and Pinot Grigio

Like so many other grapes, Pinot Gris (PEE-noh GREE) hails from France, but over the past few years, Pinot Grigio (PEE-noh GREE-zhee-yo)—the Italian name for Pinot Gris—has surpassed almost every other white wine in popularity, so much that some experts called it "the new Chardonnay." And we can understand why. Italian Pinot Grigio—probably the most widely known wine made from the Pinot Gris grape—is light in body and has decent acidity, so it's crisp and refreshing. Thus, it makes a nice aperitif and a good companion for lunch, light meals or snacks, and happy hours. And we've never heard anyone proclaim, "Wow, I really hate Pinot Grigio. It's the most horrible thing I've ever tasted." So it's definitely a crowd pleaser, making it a good pick for parties. But we think its popularity has made it almost passé. We wouldn't call it the hippest thing in the world. But before you jump on the Pinot Grigio bandwagon, make sure you try all sorts of white wines from around the world! (In case you haven't noticed, we're not the first girls to jump on any sort of a bandwagon!)

Pinot Gris, as it's known in the United States and France, is a wine of a different color, both literally and figuratively. In both countries it's fuller-bodied and tart, and tastes vaguely like apricots or other orange fruits, or even green apples. Take a stab at a Pinot Gris from California,

"Pinot gris" means "gray pinot" in French. Gray, you ask? Isn't Pinot Gris a white wine? Yes—but the skin of the grape is very dark for a white grape—hence the name.

Washington State, or Oregon, where more and more wineries are producing it. Good Pinot Gris is not cheap, but a trip to a decent wine shop should turn up some examples that won't eat up your paycheck, around $15 per bottle, maybe a tad more.

A couple more words on Italian Pinot Grigio. Sure, you can find quite cheap Pinot Grigio just about anywhere, but don't waste our money. These days, young, rising-star Italian winemakers are investing a lot of time into cultivating some really mind-blowing, lesser-known grapes indigenous to Italy, and we think they're more interesting. See page 58 for more on fun, well-made, well-priced Italian wines!

If You Like Pinot Grigio

If you like Pinot Grigio, chances are you're looking for something light, crisp, easy drinking, and refreshing. Try a Sauvignon Blanc from South Africa, or Albariño from Spain. (Albariño is crisp but fruity, with a lovely sweetish aftertaste. Find out more about it on page 65!)

What to Wear?

As little as possible. (Just kidding! We don't want you to get arrested.) Pour yourself a glass of Pinot—or order one—at brunch with your guy and his family. Wear a funky floral full skirt, strappy heels, and a sleeveless turtleneck; you'll look sexy, spring-y, *and* sophisticated.

Chenin Blanc

Chenin Blanc: It's not just for breakfast anymore. Whoops, we mean, it's not just from France anymore! In the Loire Valley region of France, this classy little grape is traditionally used to make Vouvray. Vouvrays are slightly sweetish or off-dry; but don't expect the sweetness of dessert wines. You'll find that sec Vouvrays are drier than New York City during an August blackout. (Of course, we mean that in the best possible way!)

It's actually quite likely that you'll find a reasonably priced Vouvray in a restaurant—even at a trendier-than-thou joint. Megan found herself at the bar of one of the hottest eateries in Manhattan, a place that fills up with reservations months in advance. And since we all live by the First Commandment, "Thou shalt purchase wine by the bottle whenever humanly possible," she and a friend ordered a bottle of Vouvray for around $30. Not a bad deal—especially alongside that $9 side dish of chanterelle

Is White Light?

In a word, no. Although white wines may feel "lighter" than red wines, white wines have just as much alcohol in them as their red brethren. So don't take the pale color as a license to drink more! You'll end up stumbling into expensive restaurants and ordering way more food than you need, then cabbing home at midnight. Believe us, that's a recipe for a disastrous morning after. (Um, not that we know from experience.)

mushrooms (what were we thinking?). Expect Vouvrays to be fresh, sometimes flowery, juicy, and even a bit minerally. Try them with fish, shellfish, or vegetables of any kind.

Chenin Blanc has also taken hold in South Africa, where it's sometimes known as Steen, but increasingly, South African wines made from the Chenin Blanc grape are being labeled—surprise, surprise—Chenin Blanc. (We think that just makes everyone's lives easier.) Do they call it the Cape of Good Hope because you have every right to *hope* you'll find a *good,* inexpensive Chenin Blanc from that region? Perhaps! We recently found a bottle for just $5.99 that really impressed us—and a couple of skeptics who were convinced that Chardonnay and Pinot Grigio were the only drinkable whites! Everyone loved the flavors and aromas of pears, flowers, and ripe fruits.

We like to enjoy South African Chenin Blanc as an aperitif.

If You Like Chenin Blanc

If you like Chenin Blanc superdry, try a crisp Sauvignon Blanc (and splurge on a few raw oysters while you're at it)! Or if you're more into the off-dry style, go for a Sémillon from the Pacific Northwest; it's also got a hint of sweetness and a rush of fruit.

What to Wear?

Juicy, juicy! You'll want to don something that's assertive, a little flirty, and versatile. You can't go wrong with an above-the-knee white eyelet skirt—it's feminine without being cheesy—and a tight pink sleeveless sweater. Add pink or white kitten heels or flip-flops and you'll look both relaxed and very pulled together. If the weather is frightful, layer a pink tweed blazer over a pink tee, jeans, and funky brown boots—then kick back and pour yourself a glass!

Wines You Don't Know about—but Should

It's no coincidence that the first three wines we rave about here are German or Austrian. German and Austrian wines are finally getting the love they deserve. For years, the words "German wines" conjured up images of intensely sweet and often poorly made dessert wines. But these days, there's lots more going on!

Riesling

Riesling (REESE-ling) is popping up everywhere these days. And we're thrilled! It hails from the sloped banks of German rivers, but today you can find it in cool climates around the world, including our very own Pacific Northwest and California. Don't let anyone tell you that all Rieslings are so sweet they'll make your teeth fall out. They're not. Rieslings have a very distinctive aroma, and they can smell like wildflowers, citrus, apricots, or other tropical fruits. And they go with all sorts of food, from steak (yes, we know it's a *white* wine, but some of 'em really can handle beef!) to Thai food to foie gras (now that's a match made in heaven!).

The only problem with buying Riesling is the label. (Megan speaks German and she *still* has a tough time with it.) We could confuse you with all sorts of Teutonic terminology and mind-muddling guidelines, but what fun would that be? So here are a couple easy rules of thumb.

If you're ordering Riesling in a restaurant, the cardinal rule is, *be sure to ask your server or sommelier what the wine is like*. And if you're browsing in a wine shop, look for the words *Kabinett* or *Auslese* on the label if you're looking for something light-bodied, or *Spatlese* if you want something meatier that can handle really rich food.

Next rule: The lower the alcohol content, the sweeter the wine will be, so if you want a dry Riesling, look for an alcohol content of 11 to 12 percent. Got it? Good! Once you've got that checked off your list, go for whatever's cheapest. You really can't go wrong. We think both drier and sweeter Rieslings are breathtaking, but you'll want to decide for yourself!

If You Like Riesling

Viognier's flowery aroma will remind you of Riesling, and like some Rieslings, Viognier's dry but fruity floral taste makes it seem sweet. Or sip Sémillon. Traditionally it's been blended with other whites, but we like Sémillon on its own. It's lush, rich, melon-y, and just about orgasmic.

What to Wear?

To us, Riesling always feels like a celebration. So sipping a glass is the perfect antidote to those gloomy days; no one can feel down in the dumps while drinking it! Feel like

Wine bars are the latest hip thing in just about every city, including **Boston** and **Cambridge.**

Check out **Vinalia** (101 Arch St., Boston, ☎617-737-1777), an affordable joint with a balanced selection of wines by bottle and glass.

Grab a drink with a girlfriend at **Shay's Pub and Wine Bar** (58 JFK St., Cambridge, ☎617-864-9161), and marvel that it has wine on tap. This place has been around much longer than the current wine-bar craze. With a relaxed vibe, it's just the place to stop in for a glass of yummy wine—or a beer you've never tried—and bar nibbles.

Kick it up a notch at **Troquet** (140 Boylston St., Boston, ☎617-695-9463), a restaurant run by oenophiles, where you'll love the the upscale French fare and the wine—but watch out for high prices.

Feeling a bit more swank? Stop by **Enoteca** (79 Park Plaza, Boston, ☎617-422-0008). It features almost two dozen wines by the glass—and celebrity sightings!

Go totally decadent, and pair mouthwatering desserts with a staggering selection of wine at **Finale** (30 Dunster St., Cambridge, ☎617-441-9797), where you can count on the hip staff to help you decide just what you want to splurge on!

the rock star you are by pouring a glass, and donning your glam-girl gear: an asymmetrical black tank, chandelier earrings, a frayed denim mini, and strappy heels. Talk about a pick-me-up!

Gewürztraminer

Gesundheit? No, Gewürztraminer! And we guarantee once you try this, you'll be hollering "Prost!" ("Cheers" in German, that is) and asking for another glass. Megan hates to play favorites, but this is by far her favorite white wine (and white grape). She first had it in a little café in Germany where, as a poor college student at the time, she ordered the cheapest thing on the menu. When the wine arrived, she took one sniff, jumped up, and shouted, "Oh my God, it smells like flowers!" terrifying the innocent Germans eating at the next table. But she couldn't help it. Stick your nose into a glass of Gewürz, and you'll smell rose petals, wildflowers, spices, and exotic fruit; and if it doesn't make you swoon, we'd be shocked! And if you're worried that it'll be too sweet, don't be. It smells floral and even sweet, but you'll find that most versions are much drier than you expect. A winning combination! Historically, Gewürztraminer (ge-VERTS-trah-MEEN-er) hasn't gotten much love. But now it's making up for lost time! You'll see it on wine lists in fine restaurants and hip wine bars everywhere—not just in German joints. And the great thing is, it's generally reasonably priced (although there are always exceptions to that rule). We fall back on Gewürz a lot. It's practically impossible to get a *bad* bottle of the stuff. You'll probably end up spending about $10 to $15.

The spicy little Gewürztraminer grape makes its home in the Alsace region of France, but it also makes quite a few appearances in Germany, Austria, and California. Again, we assume there must be such a thing as a nasty Gewürz, but we've never encountered one! It's particularly stellar with spicy food (it tames the spiciness a bit) such as Chinese or Indian cuisine. We also like it as a before-dinner drink, or to sip at an outdoor café on a fall afternoon.

If You Like Gewürztraminer

If you don't, we'll never talk to you again! Try a light, floral Riesling, or a flowery, peachy, honeyed Viognier.

What to Wear?

If there's one thing Gewürztraminer is not, it's shy! It makes us think of bright, fresh colors, so show off in a hot pink tube top, but keep it real by pairing it with low-riding gray pants. Megan says that her funky brown, pink, and blue-flowered shoulder bag is the spirit of Gewürz in the body of a fabulous accessory!

Grüner Veltliner

Trust us, the harder the name of a German—or in this case, Austrian—wine is to pronounce, the better it is! Grüner Veltliner (GREW-ner VELT-lee-ner) is growing in popularity, and with good reason. Like most German and Austrian wines, it's not aged in oak barrels, so you'll find that it's crisp, fruity, and often tastes likes herbs or green peppers. (So does Sauvignon Blanc. Think of Grüner as a Sauvignon Blanc with a Riesling kick!)

Although Grüner has been grown most successfully in Austria, there have been limited plantings in the neighboring countries of Hungary and Slovakia. Because Austria does not produce a whole hell of a lot of wine, it may be a bit difficult to find Grüner. If so, keep looking! Order it online. Take a road trip to a major Manhattan liquor store. Anything. Why? Because Grüner is super food-friendly, even with hard-to-match cuisines like Thai. And call her crazy, but it makes Megan want shellfish desperately. Grab an easy-drinking, refreshing Grüner for around $10, and bring it to brunch or a spring picnic. Or order in from the Thai place around the corner, and pop open a bottle!

If You Like Grüner Veltliner

You'll probably find that Sauvignon Blanc pleases your taste buds. Chances are a Sauv will have the herbal quality that also characterizes many Grüners. The most similar Sauvs also have a dash of melon scent and flavor. Or go in for a slightly sweeter Riesling, which will have some of the melon/peach flavors of an easy-drinking Grüner. Yum!

What to Wear

Something offbeat. The label on Megan's favorite Grüner sports a cute deer with its tongue sticking out. Toast to Grüner's uniqueness—and yours!—in a short plaid pleated skirt, funky-colored flats, and a tight little tee.

Sémillon

Why haven't you heard of this grape—or of its eponymous wine? Because traditionally it's been used almost solely for blending with Sauvignon Blanc. Sémillon cuts the acidity of austere Sauvignon Blanc. But nowadays, winemakers are letting Sémillon (seh-mee-YOHN) stand on its own. A wine that's 100 percent Sémillon often smells like ripe melons.

Many Australian winemakers these days blend Sémillon with Chardonnay. (It's one of the only ways Megan wants to drink Chardonnay at all!) These blended wines are usually moderately priced and can smell and taste like peach, lime, citrus, tangerine, and other summery fruits. The Chardonnay/Sémillon combo has caught on in the Pacific Northwest, so keep your eyes out for affordable versions from Washington State. The American versions might remind you of honeydew, almonds, or fresh flowers. At a recent soiree, Megan's guests decided Chardonnay/Sémillon is a great match for Brie. (But don't take our word for it— find out for yourself!)

Since Sémillon is an "emerging" grape, it might be a little tricky to find a wine that's 100 percent Sémillon, depending on where you shop. But you'll probably be able to find the Australian Chardonnay/Sémillon combo pretty easily.

If You Like Sémillon

Try an unoaked Chardonnay from South Africa (yes, they do exist, Virginia!), or a flowery German Riesling.

What to Wear?

We think Sémillon is equivalent to liquid sunshine. Wear something that'll chase the thunderstorms away. Try a sarong skirt with a funky colored tee. How about something in lemon or lime to match Sémillon's citrusy flavors? Add some high-heeled flip-flops and a trendy alfresco restaurant and you're all set.

Downtown Girl's Baked Brie

This recipe for baked Brie is so quick and simple, and the result is absolutely decadent. We love that you need only two ingredients!

5-ounce wheel of Brie

1 tube of crescent rolls (available in the refrigerated section of the supermarket)

1. Line a cookie sheet with foil.
2. Unroll the crescent roll dough into a square, without separating the rolls.
3. Place the wheel of Brie in the middle of the square. Wrap the dough around the Brie by bringing each corner of the dough to the center of the wheel and pinching the corners together. Press the dough gently but firmly around the cheese. (Don't worry if it looks less than perfect.)
4. Bake at 375 degrees for 13 to 15 minutes, till golden brown. Serve garnished with fresh fruit.

Viognier

Quick! Where does this fragrant grape call home? Take a wild guess. France? Absolutely! The Rhône River region to be exact. Of course, in these globe-shrinking days, Viognier has made its way to the New World, too—California and Australia, especially. When Megan first tasted a Viognier (vwahn-YAY) from California, she had a near-Gewürztraminer experience. Except, instead of leaping out of her chair and planting a big juicy kiss on the bartender as a sign of her deep gratitude for serving such an incredible libation, she simply sighed and sank lower in her chair. Great Viogniers smell unbelievably flowery, peachy, and even a bit like honey. Whereas wildflowery Gewürztraminers make you want to jump up and polka for joy, lush Viogniers make you want to gaze into a special someone's eyes and get all moony.

We're getting starry-eyed just thinking about it! In any event, it can be something of a challenge to find a Viognier for a reasonable price. This little grape's got a cult following! But if you do your research, you can find some well-priced examples, especially from California and Australia. (Megan just found one for $6.99, but she hasn't opened it yet. We'll get back to you!) Again, Viognier's aroma of flowers, peaches, and even tropical fruit belies the truth that Viognier is a dry wine. Try it with oily fish like salmon or tuna, or pair it with Indian takeout—Indian spices and Viognier are perfect for each other. (Even if it's a relatively dry Viognier, the perceived sweetness will help tone down heavy spices.) Or open a bottle before dinner with a platter of humus and pita.

If You Like Viognier

If Viognier is your poison of choice, try a fruity, fragrant Riesling. It and Riesling work well with similar food pairings. If you're a fan of that flowery scent, go for a wildflowery Gewürztraminer. If you love all of the above, try an exotic Torrontes from Argentina (see page 74)!

What to Wear?

Viognier makes us feel all girly. Wear whatever makes *you* feel like a natural woman! And let the pineapple-y, peachy, melon-y scents inspire you. Try a flirty, tropical-colored halter dress that flares just above the knee. Then slip on pink or yellow kitten heels and you're set!

Red-Hot White Wines!

The wide world of white wine is always changing, but here are some hot new trends to watch out for. And the best part is, most of the hot white wines you get the scoop on are $15 or less. Read on!

Italy

We don't know what it is about them, but Italian wines—especially whites—get us so excited. Is it that same *je ne sais quoi* (okay, that's French, but you get the idea) that you find in Italian men? Perhaps! Whatever it is, Megan fell in love with more than a few Italian whites at Otto, a hip Italian wine bar in Manhattan. She and her room-mate, Karen, stopped by on a Wednesday for "just a glass or two" after an art opening. But when the ever-practical Karen suggested ordering a *bottle* of Verdicchio, Megan couldn't resist. (After all, a bottle is almost always a better deal than wine by the glass!) By the time they moved on to their second bottle—this time Falanghina, a fantastically fun wine made from an indigenous Italian grape—they had befriended the restaurant's manager, Pedro, gotten in-depth knowledge of Italian cheeses from knowledgeable waiters, and consumed large quantities of gourmet pizza. How did they feel the next morning? Not great—but the point is, they became major fans of Italian white wines with just a couple of sips.

The Italian wines we're talking about go way beyond your standard Pinot Grigio or Chardonnay. These days, young Italian winemakers are focusing on some of their country's indigenous grapes, such as the ones you'll read about soon. And we think these grapes produce some absolutely fabulous wines. So why stick with just Chardonnay? Besides, you'll find the following wines on the lists of the hottest new Italian wine bars, restaurants, and wine shops around the country.

Vermentino

This grape produces really light, refreshing wines, sure to convert any avid drinker of Pinot Grigio! Like Pinot Grigio, Vermentino (vair-men-TEE-noh) is lightly fruity and very easy to drink, but also sports a bit of a grassy kick, à la Sauvignon Blanc. You'll smell pears, apples, citrus, and hints of freshly cut grass, and while it's definitely dry, you'll get a slightly sweet aftertaste. At about $10 a bottle, it's a no-brainer for white pizza, alfredo sauces, and pasta primavera, or for an aperitif before dinner.

Falanghina

If you think you don't like wine, we guarantee this one will turn you into a believer. When we say this is a "girly" wine, we mean it in the best possible way. Falanghina (fah-lahn-GEE-nah) is bright and fruity, with strong scents and aromas of peach, lime, and fresh white fruit, and even, to our surprise, bananas! And at $15 per bottle (or less), it's a real bargain. Snag a bottle now. Rumors predict it's going to be the new Pinot Grigio.

Verdicchio

Your parents might remember Verdicchio (vair-DEE-kee-oh) as a cheap, watery drink, par for the course at every inexpensive Italian restaurant. But now it's back, and it's bigger and better! Today, just like it was then, it's perfect with raw seafood—but that's not all. We love it with fried fish, vegetables tempura, and white pizza with garlic. Verdicchio is light in body, and you might smell and taste orange fruit and flowers. It's bright and lively, and just the thing to bring to an impromptu dinner with the girls on a summer night.

Moscato

We can't promise that you'll find this in every wine store near you, but do keep an eye out for it on restaurant and bar wine lists. The Moscato—"Muscat" in English—grape has a reputation for making sweet dessert wines and a sweeter sparkling wine called Asti Spumante. But Moscato (moh-SCAH-toh) is multitalented. Get your hands on a dry Muscat and you'll taste flowers such violets and lavender, hints of peach, and, sometimes, orange peel. Megan had it with a fig bruschetta and the combination was stunning.

France

The question is, what's *not* hot in France? After all, it's really the kingdom of modern winemaking. Just about every major grape can be found in one region of France or another. So when *everything's* hot, what's a girl to do?

Well, we've got a few hints for you. First, as we mentioned in our section on red wines, French wine labels, regions, and laws can be superconfusing, so if you're brand-new to wine, you really don't need to get tangled up in that kind of thing. It muddles the minds of oenophiles and connoisseurs much more experienced than you or we are. If you want to buy a great bottle of versatile, easy-drinking white wine tonight, it's a snap to find a reasonably priced Grüner Veltliner, for example, instead of scratching your head over hard-to-read French labels till you're sweating, shaking, and ready to collapse.

We can give you worthwhile shortcuts to lip-licking French whites. If you wish you could just mix Chardonnay and Sauvignon Blanc together like some kind of vinous cocktail, head straight for the white wines of the region of Graves. Labeled as such, Graves wines are blends of Sauvignon Blanc and Sémillon, and are usually aged (for not too long) in oak. The result? A "fatter" wine than bone-dry, unoaked Sauvignon Blancs.

We also like Sancerre (sahn-SAIR), which *is* bone-dry. Made from the Sauvignon Blanc grape, it smells herbal and sports an acidity that'll make your mouth water. It's divine with anything goat cheese related and fresh shellfish, too. Oh, and you won't find any oak here! Sancerre wines come in a wide range of prices, but you can find tasty versions for around $15. We think a $15 Sancerre will get you a better-quality wine than a $15 white Burgundy (French Chardonnay). And if you ask us, Sancerre goes with a wider range of foods. Besides goat cheese, it goes well with salads, poultry, and light-colored fish. And of course, we think that no matter where you find a reasonably priced Viognier, be it France, California, or the Antarctic, you should buy it, drink it, and love it.

Le Français Compliqué

French laws for labeling wine are extremely detailed and complex. However, some very recent good news is that laws have been passed allowing French winemakers to name their wines after the grape (such as Sauvignon Blanc) instead of the place the grape was grown (such as Pouilly-Fumé). But bear in mind that in France a wine can be labeled as Sauvignon Blanc (or Merlot, etc.) only if the wine was made using *only* Sauvignon Blanc grapes. Therefore, it is always in the wine buyer's best interest to ask when purchasing wine, lest she misses out on the great wine from the Entre-Deux-Mers area that is 98 percent Sauvignon Blanc even though it may not say Sauvignon Blanc anywhere on the label.

I'd Like My White Burgundy to Go, Please!

Recently, many restaurants in France took part in an experiment—doggy bags for customers' unfinished bottles of wine! Customers get a "kit" with a new cork and a device to prevent oxidation, so they can recork their wine and get it home still fresh. Now consumers who'd rather not waste wine don't need to polish off the whole bottle at the restaurant. Who knows? Maybe someday the Downtown Girl will be able to get a nice glass of vino to go as easily as she gets a Starbucks. (Oh, and can I get some fries with that?)

Germany and Austria

It's taken awhile, but we Americans are finally figuring out that pudgy, way-too-oaky wines like the average Chardonnay in a box are not God's gift to wine-kind. Worldwide, the trend is toward crisp, clean whites that show off the natural flavors of the grape—and that go wonderfully with food. (Just ask the Italians! See page 58.)

This sure isn't news to German and Austrian winemakers. Most of their wines are aged in stainless steel barrels, which impart no additional flavor to the wine at all; they just let the grapes get their groove on. Sounds good to us! Prepare to be surprised by spicy Gewürztraminers and floored by the melony peachiness of some Grüner Veltliners.

Sylvaner

Why haven't you heard of this grape if it's so darn hot? Because until recently it was blended only in small amounts

Bacon-Wrapped Dates

No, we're not talking about that sort of beefcake. This is the easiest, most foolproof appetizer Megan knows, and at parties, everyone devours them before you can say "Pinot Noir." Bacon-wrapped dates are salty, sweet, decadent, and addictive.

1-pound package of bacon

16 dried dates

1. Lay 16 slices of raw bacon on a cookie sheet lined with foil, and bake at 400 degrees for around 10 minutes, turning once after 5 minutes.

2. When the bacon is thoroughly cooked but not brittle, remove it from the cookie sheet with a fork and lay it on paper towels briefly.

3. Roll a slice of bacon around a date, working carefully because the bacon is still hot. Secure with a toothpick. Repeat for each of the dates.

4. Place the dates on an oven-safe plate and pop in the oven for a couple more minutes so they're piping hot. Serve immediately. They'll be gone in seconds!

with other whites. But now, German and Austrian winemakers are popping out with 100 percent Sylvaners to quite a bit of acclaim. Sylvaner is similar to Grüner Veltliner but a bit sweeter, making it a great cocktail wine. Be prepared to pay for a Sylvaner, because you won't find many $10 versions. If you spot one on a restaurant wine list, that's a sure sign that the place is *echt* (authentic) vino-savvy.

Grüner Veltliner

It's really the most important white grape in Austria these days (okay, Austria's not that big, but still). And it's not always a snap to find, but when you do, the quality is fantastic for the price. Keep your eyes open for these little diamonds in the rough!

Riesling

Some things never change. Riesling's always been the hallmark grape of Germany, and not much has changed about that—but the quality of Rieslings exported to the United States certainly has. Sure, there're bound to be some lemons. Wine snobs will certainly scoff at this, but when we're in a rush, we just grab the cheapest one we can find—as long as it's not a dessert Riesling—and hope for the best. The great thing is, that tactic rarely disappoints us. Nothing's certain but death and taxes, but honestly, we've never had an undrinkable German Riesling.

Spain

These days, *tapas* is the word on the street. We love it! What better way to get together with friends after hours than sharing a few bottles of wine (or sangria), and sampling lots of "little dishes"? Next time, skip the red wines of Spain. Yes, we know they're great, but did you know Spain's whites are equally as tempting? Historically, they've been overlooked, but no more! Today they're getting much-deserved credit for being refreshing on their own, and great companions for food.

At a recent tasting, we tried Albariño for the first time, and we were hooked. It really is a crowd pleaser. Peaches, apples, and melon, oh my! Albariño smells like a fresh summer fruit salad, and has a slightly sweet aftertaste (but, rest assured, it's not a "sweet" wine!). It's delicious with tapas of all kinds, including anything having to do with chorizo sausage and spicy potatoes (*patatas bravas*). And it's a great match with paella, too. Absolutely bring it to a Labor Day barbecue. You can nab a bottle for around $11.

Portugal

Portugal has been producing wine for hundreds of years, but until recently, the only kind of Portuguese wine seen on the American market was port (a sweet fortified wine). Not so these days! Portuguese wines are becoming more and more popular, especially those made from one of the many

Mix and Mingle

Ladies, we operate under the following maxim: If a guy wants to buy you a drink, why shouldn't you let him? Of course, we would never endorse hanging out at bars trying to snag sugar daddies, but hey, why refuse a nice gesture? Next time you and a buddy or two are at a wine bar, do your best to sit at the bar, not at a table. That way, you'll meet more people (including men who might want to chat over a glass of wine), and chances are you'll get better service (you'll be right in the bartender's line of sight). It also gives you a chance to wow a potential Mr. Big with your wine savvy!

What's the Deal with Corkage Fees?

Sure, you may be paying a lot for that plate of Chilean sea bass or pasta with shaved black truffles, but wine and spirits are where the real money is for restaurant (and bar) owners. With standard markups on alcoholic beverages of 100 percent to 400 percent above wholesale price, restaurants lose money if you bring your own bottle of wine. Some upscale restaurants, therefore, charge a corkage fee, usually between $10 and $25, per bottle. Sounds like a rip-off, but even with the fee, bringing your wine is almost always cheaper.

grapes native to the country. And you won't find a whole lot of budget busters among them. Some of our favorite whites include Vinho Verde (VEEN-yoh VAIRD), which means "green wine." Is it called "green" after its motherland, the lush Minho region of Portugal? No one's certain. The most common belief is that verde refers to the wine's youthfulness, because the grapes are picked early and the wine is drunk young. Wherever its origin, this grape by any other name would taste as dry! At prices you can't buy a pair of socks for—starting at $6 or $7—why not stock up? Vinho Verde 's almost sparkling, smells and tastes like citrus fruits, and is so crisp it almost snaps in your mouth. We like it any time of year, but believe it's one of the all-time best libations for a sultry, sticky summer day. Try it with shellfish of all kinds, done any way you like 'em.

Then there's the lesser-known Arinto (ah-REEN-toe) grape. Indigenous to Portugal, it sports fresh, creamy lemony scents, hints of green apple, and you can't go wrong by pairing it with veggies of all sorts, or anything that swims.

Other European Regions

Thought the world of whites ended with Italy? Think again! Greece and Eastern Europe are producing some lip-licking whites these days that are truly good to the last drop. Prices vary, you can find something fab at a price that'll make you stop in your stiletto-heeled tracks.

Hungary

Open to the back of the most recent issue of a hoity-toity wine magazine, and the only Hungarian wines you'll see are the sweet dessert wines made in the Tokaj (toh-KAI) region. They're labeled "Tokaji" (adding the "i" makes the word possessive, as in "Tokaj's wine") but we usually call them Tokays. Although these are often extraordinary once-in-a-lifetime wines, you'll see them clocking in at prices like $624 (yes, that's in U.S. dollars!) for just 500 milliliters (15 ounces), or just about two-thirds the size of a regular bottle of wine. Unless you're Ivana Trump or married to Bruce Wayne, Tokajis in this price range probably won't be on your agenda. However, while traditionally expensive, Tokajis, like wines from other regions, vary immensely in price. Most good wine shops stock an affordable Tokaji. (See page 169 for more on the splurge-worthy variety!)

In addition, many restaurants now offer Tokaji as a dessert wine for $10 to 15 a glass. (Find out more about

Tokaji in Chapter 6.) You can also look to the lesser-known and more reasonably priced wines of Hungary. We love the Irsai Olivér grape because wines made from it taste like close cousins of our all-time favorites, Gewürztraminer and Riesling. Irsai Olivér wines smell like tropical fruit and flowers, and taste a little spicy. At $10 a bottle, we think it's a steal.

The aforementioned sweet dessert wines are made from the Furmint grape, but dry wines made from the same grape are increasing in popularity. Many Furmint wines are as crisp as apples and even a little smoky. They are terrific with smoked Gouda and soft creamy cheeses like Brie or Camembert, and with all sorts of grilled vegetables. Look for "Tokaji Furmint" on the label. If the wine's in a regular-size wine bottle, chances are it's a dry wine, but double-check with the wine shop staff to be sure.

Greece

Okay, the Greeks practically invented wine thousands of years ago. But in the history of modern winemaking, Greek wines haven't gotten a whole lot of attention. All that's changing now, because Greek winemakers stepped up to the plate with affordable, quality wines that are drinkable, food friendly, and fun. We love Moschofilero (moss-koh-FEE-leh-roh), which'll run you only $9, a steal for this superlight, aromatic white that's fragrant with apples and pears. (It's another "girly in a good way" pick!) Moschofilero is the top-selling wine in Greece, and we suggest it's a great alternative to that other ubiquitous standard—Chardonnay. Pair it with just about anything, including Thai food.

If you can get your hands on a wine made from the Assyrtiko grape, by all means get it! It's a great white wine and a wonderful alternative to Chardonnay. Megan was lucky enough to spend hours over an incredible Greek dinner (and wine, of course!) with the chief oenologist—that's winespeak for Wine Boss—of Boutari, a top Greek winery. He introduced her to Boutari's version of the Assyrtiko wine. The only way to describe it is the best "Chardonnay" you've ever had. And that's saying quite a bit, because you know how we feel about the average Chard! Amazing! Mind you, not as amazing as the flaming cheese, but delicious nonetheless.

United States

Pretty much every type of grape you can imagine is grown somewhere in the United States, and you can find an American version of almost any type of wine, from Gewürztraminer to Pinot Gris to Chardonnay. American winemakers are really expanding their horizons these days. We think it's great! We could write an entire book on America's many wine-producing regions, from the North Fork of Long

Today, Paris—tomorrow, the world! The wine bar trend has swept through America, and it's even catching on in Greece! There's one difference, though: Greek tipplers enjoy their wine in single-serve bottles, similar to the ones you see on airplanes. We think it's a great idea; that way you get a fresh bottle with every glass!

Island to Napa Valley—but to save you time and energy, we'll highlight just a few great wines from the Etats Unis.

California produces massive quantities of wine, and that can be a little overwhelming. Where to start? Well, it won't surprise you to hear that we skip most of those $6 bottles of California Chardonnay. Boring! And chances are their quality won't be stellar. If you're a Viognier addict like us, look for some well-priced versions from California. You won't have to pay top dollar to get your fix! And strangely enough, we recently had a delicious, lightly flowery, spicy Gewürztraminer from the Mendocino region of California, which is far north enough to give the grape the cool climate it needs. Call us crazy, but we get Sémillons wherever we can find them, and, although there aren't a lot of them, you'll see a few nice examples popping up in California. Try one!

Seeking Sémillon? Look for some bargain-priced versions from Washington State, especially the Columbia Valley area. Around $15 a pop—no need to spend more—Washington Sémillons can deliver a good dose of flowers, citrus fruit, and spice. They're certainly never shy!

When it comes to Oregon, you'll definitely want to check out Pinot Gris, especially from the Willamette Valley region. Oregon Gris (those in the know leave off the "Pinot") are often tart, apple-y, and refreshing with "green" flavors, and you won't have to spend more than $10 to $15 to get a good one.

The Finger Lakes area of upstate New York is *the* place for Rieslings and Gewürztraminer. The region's cooler climate makes the grapes feel right at home.

∿ SEATTLE ∿

Because the Pacific Northwest is a such an up-and-coming, exciting wine region, is it a surprise that **Seattle** sports great wine bars and wine-focused restaurants?

Grab a glass or two at **Impromptu Wine and Art Bar** (4235 E. Madison Street, ☎206-860-1569). Every couple of months, the top-notch wine list focuses on a different winemaking region from around the world, such as the Willamette Valley region of Oregon, or the Bordeaux region of France. The solicitous staff will answer all your questions and make you feel right at home, whether you're a seasoned Bacchanalian or a wine rookie.

Feeling flush? Check out **Kaspar's Restaurant and Wine Bar** (19 W. Harrison Street, ☎206-298-0123), where you'll find world-class food and wine at prices that'll leave you smiling. And the mind-blowing wine list is easy to navigate. Don't miss the daily happy hour at the bar. You'll find fab drink specials, and appetizers are half price!

South Africa

Relatively new to the wine world, South African wines were shunned by consumers until recently because of South Africa's former apartheid policy. But even if you wanted to buy a bottle of South African wine, not many varieties were imported into the United States in the first place. Today, South Africa is a rising star in the world of wine, so don't be afraid to try a bottle! Chenin Blanc, also known as Steen, is one of its most popular South African whites. Fruity, yet definitely dry, it'll remind you of green apples and vanilla, or possibly pears and flowers. And you'll find versions as low as $6. Look for Sauvignon Blancs from South Africa, too. They're full of citrus fruit, and they're delicious with grilled chicken or seafood.

South America

Although South American countries are mostly known for their red wines, their whites are emerging. Happily, the quality of their whites is generally good, and the price is definitely user-friendly. Why? Simply because South American whites haven't been discovered yet. Of course, that won't last forever, so take advantage of it now, before prices go up. Be a trendsetter!

Chile

We're in luck! The white grapes that do so well in Chile just happen to be two of the most popular grapes in the United States: Chardonnay and Sauvignon Blanc. Great Chards often hail from Chile's Maipo region, and many great Sauvignons call Chile's Rapel region home. The Casablanca region of Chile is also widely acknowledged as a top region for producing white wines. Buying white wines from Chile is like being the first to find out about the hottest club in town, then sliding past the velvet rope without paying a cover, to find free bottle service once you get to your table. (And a bevy of hot waiters to cater to your every whim.)

That is, you can hardly believe your luck! Chardonnays and Sauvignons from Chile are usually in the $6 to $12 range, which means you should definitely stock up for parties any time of year. Chilean Chardonnays tend to be oaky, so if that's your thing, play on, player. If not, you'll just have to do a lot of drinking to figure out which ones you like! Also, look for Chardonnay/Chenin Blanc blends, which are typically a lot less on the oaky side. When it comes to Sauvignon Blanc, you can expect tropical fruit scents and flavors similar to what you'd find in a New Zealand version. Our advice? Get 'em while they're hot!

Argentina

Argentina is a major player when it comes to reasonably priced Malbec, a red wine, but keep this in mind: If you ever come across a little-known wine called Torrontes, order a glass (or buy a bottle) pronto. To get it, you might have to find an especially well-stocked wine bar or a specialty wine shop, but it's worth the effort. How can we describe exciting, aromatic Torrontes? Perhaps as a combination of a

---

Useless Wine Fact to Use When Showing Off

When you taste a little bit of effervescence in a wine that's not officially designated as sparkling, it's because a dash of naturally occurring carbon dioxide got stuck—or suspended—in the wine during fermentation. It's not a winemaking flaw. In fact, we consider it an extra treat, because bubbles feel so good in your mouth.

Chic Sipping

Next time you splurge on yourself (or register for wedding gifts!) go for stemless wineglasses, or wine "tumblers." Yes, you heard right! These all-purpose glasses help maintain the wine's integrity, and they're easier to store (and, we think, hold). Visit *www.riedel.com*, click on O-Riedel Collection, and you'll find tumblers designed for just about any wine you can imagine drinking.

relatively dry Riesling and a dash of Gewürztraminer with a spritz of near-effervescence. All in all, it's tons of fun, and it's relatively cheap. A bottle will run you about $12 to $14, and a glass at a wine bar will run you around $6.

Australia

Ah, the Australian wine revolution! The Land Down Under hasn't been a vinous superpower for very long. In fact, until about thirty years ago, most of its wines were sweet and fortified, like dessert wines. Then Shiraz exploded onto the scene, putting Australia on the wine lover's map—followed by white grapes such as Chardonnay, Riesling, Sémillon, and Viognier. You'll find high-quality Australian Rieslings in the $15 region. They're often apple-y and bone dry, and many come with screw caps, so you can even screw the corkscrew. Try these superdry Rieslings with shrimp cocktail sans the marinara sauce, or with clams on the half shell.

The Margaret River region in Western Australia is tossing out some better Chardonnays these days. A few of them actually aren't aged in oak—miracle of miracles!—and you'll be able to find a few easily for around $11 to $13. Having trouble? Ask your wine shop owner for an Australian Chardonnay that's not oaky (assuming the non-oaky type is your preference). Or skim the descriptions on the back labels of the bottles, and skip anything that touts it as "oaky," "vanilla," "butterscotch," or "buttery."

But we think the best choice is the Chard/Sémillon combination. In Australia, this blockbuster blend often smells and tastes of pears or peaches, and citrus fruit such as tangerines or limes. You won't get that same cloying oakyness you find in so many Chardonnays around the world.

Viognier's cult following has extended halfway around the world. Look for Aussie versions, though they may be a little tougher to find!

New Zealand

The word on the proverbial street in New Zealand is, Sauvignon Blanc! This island's producing boatloads of the stuff at prices ranging from nice 'n' cheap to the price of a pair of Prada stilettos. (Okay, that's a slight exaggeration. Nothing's *that* expensive! But you catch our drift.) New Zee Sauvignons don't have the cat-pee scent—er, we mean, that fragrance of gooseberries—that many French versions do. Instead, they show off with tropical and citrus scents of passion fruit, kiwi, lime, and grapefruit, and the classic

Should You Put Ice Cubes in Your White Wine?

Absolutely not! First, they'll probably chill your wine too much. Second, melting ice will water it down. Both outcomes distort the flavor and feel of the wine. If you're worried about drinking too much, too fast, alternate sips of wine with sips of water. And please, if you're adding ice to a wine to mask the taste, don't drink the wine in the first place. After all, Jesus turned water into wine, not a white-wine spritzer, for a reason!

Sauvignon-y undertones of herbs and freshly cut grass. It's just as much of a crowd pleaser as that old standby, Chardonnay, and a much better match for a range of foods.

Sure enough, that loveable grape Riesling has made its way around the world, and stopped in New Zealand for a visit. (We hope a long one!) Expect to see some light, fruity Rieslings that often smell gently of pears and apricots for around $12 to $15. Yummy with salads. And if you're a fan of the bright-orange fruit that's a hallmark of Pinot Gris, check out a couple from the Marlborough region of New Zealand. Good ones will run you about $15.

Japan

You're thinking: Wait a minute, I've never heard of Japanese wine before. Hello, sushi lovers—you've had Japan's sake (SAH-kee), or rice wine! Sake has been around for thousands of years, but a lot of Americans tend to give it the hairy eyeball because of language barriers. ("I have no clue what this label says. How do I know what I'm buying?") These days, sake is showing up in hot bars and restaurants everywhere, not just sushi joints. Erase those memories of getting trashed on hot, cheap sake while shoveling back all kinds of teriyaki. Today's sake is nothing like that. It's popular with restaurateurs because it has good, crisp acidity—and it solves the age-old question, what on earth do I serve with Asian cuisine?

Try sake with any kind of raw fish, sushi dipped in wasabi, or other Asian-influenced dishes like black-sesame-crusted salmon. But skip the fatty stuff, like steak, bacon, or heavy cream sauces, because sake just can't stand up to it. So where's the best place to start with sake? A great Japanese restaurant, where the server or sommelier will be able to guide you around the list.

Best Buzz for Your Buck:
Top 10 White Wines Under $10

Are you looking for drinkable, quality whites that'll still leave you with enough cash to hit a few sample sales? Look no further than these can't-miss tipples. It's pretty easy to find versions of these white wines for under ten bucks in just about any wine shop:

1. Vinho Verde from Portugal
2. Chenin Blanc from South Africa

3. Albariño from Spain
4. Grüner Veltliner from Austria
5. Torrontes from Argentina
6. Chardonnay from South Africa
7. Moschofilero from Greece
8. Falanghina from Italy (okay, this one's closer to $15, but it's worth the extra few bucks!)
9. Irsai Olivér from Hungary
10. Sémillon/Chardonnay blend from Australia

At prices like these you can even start building your own wine cellar!

Throwing the Best Wine-and-Cheese Soiree Ever!

If you're looking to throw a low-stress shindig, or if you decide to invite a bunch of buddies over last minute on a Friday night, why not make it a wine-and-cheese party? Believe us, it's a laid-back, relatively inexpensive, and very cool way to host a party. Plus, as the host, you'll actually have time to mingle with your guests and enjoy a glass of wine yourself, instead of running back and forth from the kitchen! Here are a few tips for making your wine-and-cheese soiree an event to remember:

● Whenever you're serving alcohol to guests, be sure to serve plenty of food! You don't want anyone to feel sick or lightheaded. And more is always better than less; you'll have plenty of leftovers the next day!

● Make sure you've got lots of water, soda, and club soda on hand for any teetotalers—especially designated drivers—and the drinkers, too. Drinking lots of nonalcoholic liquids while you're imbibing will prevent that hangover!

● You'll probably want to serve both red and white wines and a variety of cheeses (Skip the bags of cubed Cheddar!) to satisfy everyone's taste.

● Always serve white wines before red ones, and milder-flavored cheeses before stronger ones. You should go from softer flavors to more robust ones, to keep strong flavors from ruining your taste buds for delicate flavors.

● Wines with a little sweetness are perfect with salty cheese (and foods of all kinds); they contrast well with one another.

● Champagnes—or good, dry sparkling wines—go wonderfully with just about everything from fresh fruit to Brie to hard cheeses like Parmigiano-Reggiano, not to mention chocolate!

● But wait! Light red wines such as Pinot Noir or Beaujolais Nouveau are also good matches with Brie and Camembert.

● Pair fresh cheeses, such as fresh mozzarella or cream cheese, with lighter, fruitier wines.

● Blue cheeses of all kinds are traditionally matched with port or sherry, but Sauvignon Blanc will do the trick, too.

● Hard cheeses like Parmigiano-Reggiano or Asiago are stellar with New-World Cabernet Sauvignons.

● Goat cheese demands Sauvignon Blanc, whether the wine is from New Zealand, South Africa, or France (where it'll be known as Pouilly-Fumé or Sancerre).

● Blue Stilton and port are a classic, winning combination—and totally indulgent. Sounds old-fashioned, but this combination is a truly decadent classic. Serve it at the end of the night!

How to be a flawless hostess? Simple—follow these four commandments:

1. **Always make sure no one's glass is empty.** Unless your guest wants it to be!
2. **Make time to chat with all of your guests.** Try not to get caught in a corner gabbing with your best bud the whole time.
3. **Never cry over spilled wine!** If a partygoer spills or drops her glass, make a joke about it and clean it up cheerfully—even if she broke one of your $30 Riedel glasses. She feels bad enough over her faux pas already.
4. **Never, *ever*, let your guests drive home after a glass too many.** This is the (über) commandment that takes precedence in every Downtown Girl's hostess-with-the-mostest guide. We're all about imbibing with gusto—as long as it's done responsibly. 'Nuff said!

Whenever Your Heart Desires!

Well, Downtown Girl, now you know when to drink white wine—whenever you want! It's not just for drinking from cardboard boxes, or to cool down in summer. And white wines are every bit as classy as their red cousins. You're expanding your horizons way beyond what you know, you've become enchanted by the wildflower scent of Gewürztraminer, and you've been seduced by the oh-so-crispness of a great Sauvignon Blanc. Makes us thirsty just thinking about it! So grab a few friends, some bottles of white you haven't tried yet, and let the games begin!

Chapter Three

Isn't That
Just Grape?
Red, Red Wine

Yes, we know, we know. It makes you feel so fine and keeps you rockin' all of the time. And with good reason: The tannins in red wine help give that full-bodied feel in your mouth. Reds feel richer and warmer than whites. Chalk that up to the tannin, too. White wines are all coolness and refinement; reds are rich, lusty, and a bit seductive. Think Grace Kelly versus Sophia Loren.

"Rich," "warm," "full"—the adjectives are going right to our heads already! And a red is never just a red. Red wines can be light and fruity, like Beaujolais or New-World Syrahs, or they can be earthy, deep, and so red they're almost black, like Petite Syrah or some Bordeaux. There's really something for every taste, so it's time for you to revise the notion that "red wine is too heavy."

There's just something about red wine that's downright sexy. Is it the color, ranging from a pale ruby to an inky purple-black? Is it that it's a great match with decadent fare? (Think a muscular, hunky Cabernet with a chargrilled steak, a smoky Pinot Noir with crisp bacon, or even a lush port with dark chocolate.) Is it red wine's arresting aromas, evocative of black fruit, chocolate, tobacco, earth, spice, and maybe a little bit of mystery? We say it's all of the above! We like to think of reds as the Heathcliffs of wine: dark, seductive, and always surprising.

Keep reading, and you'll learn why it's perfectly fine not to drink Merlot, which cheeses to pair with which reds, which wines are gaining popularity in hot vino-focused bars around the country, and much more. We begin our journey with the major red grapes.

Merlot

If Sigmund Freud (or someone much cuter) appeared at your dinner table to play free association over a steak dinner, he'd probably ask, "What's the first word that comes to mind when I say, 'red wine'?" And we bet you a swimming pool brimming with Cristal that you'd say, "Merlot." If you said "Nebbiolo" or "Gamay," brava—chances are, you're one well-rounded, red-drinking dame. If not, never fear! It's not your fault. You're the victim of a worldwide conspiracy. People drink Merlot for the same reasons they buy their jeans at that ubiquitous clothing store that rhymes with "rap" and their shoes at the shoe-ery that rhymes with "Wine Best." And those reasons are familiarity, ease, and the idea that people know what they're getting. (And that's fair enough, but you won't learn a whole hell of a lot that way.)

Grown in the Bordeaux region of France, the west coast of the United States, and a bit in Italy, Spain, Chile, and

South Africa (to name a few), Merlot is soft—or "plush," to use a bit of winespeak—which means the tannins in it generally won't strip paint off a car. And Merlot is relatively inoffensive. It often tastes like dark red fruits (such as black cherries and or plums) and perhaps chocolate. Merlot won't screw up beef, roast pork, duck, or other heavy, dark meats, so stick with those when you're serving Merlot. Otherwise, don't serve it and try a different red wine. If you've always thought you weren't a red wine sort of gal, it's possible you're just not used to those pesky tannins. Next time you're faced with a glass of red—be it Cabernet, Pinot Noir, or Zinfandel—try it with food, preferably something fatty. (Great excuse to throw calorie concerns to the wind!) Fat softens the tannins in red wine, so it won't feel nearly as puckery in your mouth.

Let's face it, Merlot is a little—how shall we put it?—five-minutes-ago.com. And that, our Downtown Girl, is something you are not. Go ahead, grab a random bottle of some vaguely French, $10 Merlot off the first shelf you see at the liquor store and bring it to your wine-fearing in-laws. They won't mind. They'll just drink it. But you and we both know there's so much more to wine than the status quo! Thus, we propose something radical, something bold: Feel

Tannin: sounds like something akin to food poisoning. "I'm suffering from tannin today, Boss. I won't be able to make it in." Not so—unless you're suffering from a red-wine-induced hangover! Tannin is a naturally occurring compound found in the skins of red grapes. It's what gives red wine its body. Know how your teeth and gums feel dry after a sip of red? Bingo—tannin.

free to skip it. There are as many bad bottles of Merlot to be had in America's liquor stores and wine shops as there are scary men in singles bars. So let's put this grape on the back burner for now. Not that *all* Merlot is bad! It's just that it can be pretty tough to find a good one. Plus, instead of drinking your Old Faithful, why not try something new? If you must, try one from Spain or Chile; the prices will be low, the quality, spiffy, and at least you're getting out of France and into the rest of the world!

If You Like Merlot

Yes, we'll forgive you! If you like Merlot you're probably a girl who wants a medium-bodied wine—that is, one that's not too light, not too heavy, with "soft" tannins. So try a light, fruity Beaujolais Nouveau, or a Pinot Noir, another lighter red that's supersmooth, but powerful.

What to Wear?

If you're drinking Merlot, you're feeling chill. You're not worried about stilettos or lipstick; you just want to kick back with something you know. Go for it! Sip a glass in stretchy, hip-hugging black pants (maybe they're your yoga pants!) and a tight tank. And feel free to wear sneakers.

Cabernet Sauvignon

Oh, baby. Cabs! Forget Merlot. Cabernet Sauvignon is the most popular grape in the world today, and that makes us very happy. Why? Because if Cab were a guy, not a grape,

To Blend, or Not to Blend?

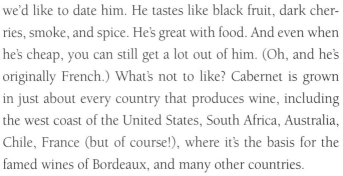

That was our question when we first began to learn about wine. Isn't a wine that's 100 percent Cabernet Sauvignon better than a wine that's, say, 70 percent Cab and 30 percent Merlot—just the way you'd probably prefer a sweater that's 100 percent wool to one that's a wool/polyester blend? *Mais non!* Winemakers often blend different grapes to create a balanced wine. For example, soft Merlot balances out hefty Cab nicely. Yin and yang. Heaven and earth. Now we're getting carried away....

we'd like to date him. He tastes like black fruit, dark cherries, smoke, and spice. He's great with food. And even when he's cheap, you can still get a lot out of him. (Oh, and he's originally French.) What's not to like? Cabernet is grown in just about every country that produces wine, including the west coast of the United States, South Africa, Australia, Chile, France (but of course!), where it's the basis for the famed wines of Bordeaux, and many other countries.

You thought we were kidding when we likened Cab to a dateable guy, but some of the words used to describe Cab really do apply to men, too! (Especially men in their twenties.) "Hefty," "muscular," "robust," and even "brutish." And like the best men, the best Cabs soften with age—becoming "polished" wines with "character" you'll want to keep for the long haul. (Moral of the story? Men in their twenties just aren't ripe yet!)

Not that you can't date around first. You should. Snag some Cabs to drink now, not to age. For that purpose, we

Whether you're going to a penthouse dinner party or bringing a wine to a chum's wine-and-cheese event, **Astor Wines & Spirits** (12 Astor Place at Lafayette Street, ☎212-674-7500, *www.astoruncorked.com*) is the shrine to vino (and booze!) in New York City. Reasonable prices, a colossal selection, and the most helpful staff ever make it a no-brainer.

like to try more nontraditional, New-World Cabs—that is, those not made in Europe—just for fun. But there's no need to spend all the cash you were saving for that little Louis Vuitton bag; you just have to know where to look! You'll find some great bargains from Chile and South Africa especially, and they're popping up at very reasonable prices from Washington State, too.

There's one thing that Cabernet is not, and that's shy. This means when it comes to food, you're not pairing this puppy with delicate fish or anything in a light cream sauce. Pour a glass or two with a char-grilled steak or lamb chops—or be a tad extravagant, and have a glass next to a cheeseburger with all the fixings.

If You Like Cabernet

You're definitely not a shrinking violet, and neither is your taste in wine! You want high-impact wines, and again Pinot Noir fits the bill. Try one from the west coast of the United States, which produces a wine thick with dark cherries, that can even be earthy or spicy (although not as heavy as a Cab). Or grab an Australian Shiraz, which will be packed with dark fruit (blueberries, blackberries, black cherries) and spice, often at prices that won't hurt a bit.

What to Wear?

Because it's so full-bodied, Cabernet is a great cold-weather choice. Sip it while wearing a sexy suede jacket over a lacey camisole or shell. Or go casual, topping boot-cut dark jeans with a black turtleneck sweater for a laid-back look that's as classic as a Cab!

Pinot Noir

We don't like to play favorites, but this may be Megan's favorite grape. Why? Because its juice creates wines that are relatively light-bodied, but pack a mean punch of aroma and flavor. Stick your nose into a glass of Pinot (to sound like an expert, leave off the "Noir"), and your nose might be treated to scents of spice, earth, smoke, mushroom, woods (think of the smell of autumn leaves on the forest floor), and of course, a good dose of dark or dried cherries. Now that's a very sexy combination! We think Pinot is the most seductive wine there is. If your new guy invites you over for a romantic dinner and you're looking for the perfect wine to prove your good (or naughty!) intentions, Pinot is it. Skip the stilettos and the Wonderbra! Pinot's earthy, smoky scents will put both you and him in the mood—and fast.

Pinot's origin is the Burgundy region of France, where it becomes—surprise, surprise—red Burgundy. (Remember that the French name their wines after the place the grape is grown, not after the name of the grape itself.) Red burgundies are famous the world over for the way they reflect their terroir—their growing conditions, including the soil,

Wine and Cheese: Some Rules of Thumb

Always start out with something mild and build up to the most flavorful cheeses. In making your selections, remember that wines and cheeses from the same region tend to go wonderfully together, but you should experiment, of course. Food (and not just cheese) and wine can be paired in two ways: They can either complement each other or contrast with each other. What does that mean? Your pink polo shirt complements (matches) your pink and gray miniskirt, while your classic, crisp white top contrasts with (sets off) your black suit skirt perfectly. Similarly, a buttery Chardonnay is a nice match with a soft, buttery cheese like triple-crème Brie.

climate, and weather—and for being a perfect match with French fare. But good red Burgundy is tough to find (and when you do find it, it tends to be pricey), which is why it's a good idea to stick with Pinots from California, Oregon, and Washington State. New Zealand is also producing more and more Pinot; in fact, there's more Pinot in New Zealand than any other grape! While good Pinots aren't dirt cheap, you'll find some nice ones in the $10 to $15 range—and they're definitely worth the money.

Pinot is fantastic on its own or with just about any food at all. It's the varietal that broke the "red wine is for red meat—white-wine is for fish" mold. Try it with salmon or fresh tuna or pair it with poultry, especially the dark meat, and see for yourself. You really can't go wrong. Bring it to your coworker's barbecue or to your in-laws at

Thanksgiving, and be sure to order it at a restaurant if you're having the salmon with dill, but your boyfriend's having the filet mignon. Pinot's a guaranteed crowd pleaser!

If You Like Pinot

If you like Pinot, chances are you want a medium-bodied wine that's exciting but very drinkable. You'll like the light, fresh fruitiness of a Beaujolais Nouveau from France, or a fun, outgoing Zinfandel full of cherry and blueberry flavor from California.

What to Wear?

Alluring, come-hither Pinot demands an equally sexy outfit. But you don't want to reveal too much. You'll want to leave something to the imagination! When Megan's drinking Pinot (which is more often than not), she slides on a strappy-yet-simple black tank from DKNY (thank you, sales at Saks!) over a pair of sleek black pants. It's a no-brainer. Wearing all black is slimming, makes you look oh-so-sophisticated and mysterious, and if you spill a bit of Pinot on your clothes, no one will notice!

Shiraz, Syrah

Think fast: What's hotter than Jude Law on a tin roof? Why, Shiraz, of course! Over the last ten years or so, Shiraz has been *the* buzzword when it comes to New-World wines. And its popularity hasn't let up a bit! Today it rivals even Merlot's bestseller status—and with good reason. Why?

Because we can sum up Shiraz's charms in one word: Yum! Spicy and full of ripe-berry flavors (think strawberry, fresh cherries, raspberries), it's tons of fun to drink. It's just the thing to bring to a girls' night in, or to sip on a warm summer evening before throwing some chicken on the grill. We can just about guarantee that everyone will love it.

What's in a name? "Shiraz" (pronounced she-RAHZ) and "Syrah" (pronounced see-RAH) certainly don't sound French, do they? Here's why. Legend has it that the Syrah grape was brought to France from Persia nearly 1,000 years ago. Then in the early 1800s Syrah made its way to Australia where today it is the country's most widely planted red grape. The Australians call their grape Shiraz, embracing the original pronunciation. But no matter how you say it, Shiraz and Syrah are absolutely the same grape.

The French have Syrah to thank for some of their best (and often most expensive) wines, including Châteauneuf-du-Pape, Hermitage, and Côte Rôtie. It's pretty hard to find stellar examples of these wines at price points you can easily afford. Instead, snag a bottle of inexpensive Côtes du Rhône. At $10 to $15—the price of, say, a denim miniskirt or cute shirt on sale!—you won't need to invest a lot of cash to give it a shot.

And of course, there're lots of good values to be had in Shiraz from the Land Down Under, Shiraz's second home. It's hard to go wrong with Aussie Shiraz; we've liked almost every bottle in the $8 to $15 range. Keep an eye out for some particularly snazzy values from the Pemberton and Great Southern regions. Shiraz, Australian or otherwise, is an especially good bet, since it can fit in just about

Wine for the Masses

You'd do anything for a bargain, right? Stand in line at the sample sale for a full two hours just to snag Chanel lipstick for $3, shove your best friend out of the way for that Armani Exchange top marked down to $19.99—even buy red wine from that scary No Refunds barrel at the liquor store. How to salvage cheap red wine? Turn it into sangria! Slice apples, oranges, lemons, and limes, and put them in a pitcher with ice. Toss in about a half cup of brandy, add the less-than-perfect bottle of wine, and you've got a fruity libation that's fabulous for summer sipping.

anywhere, from a backyard barbecue to the most refined of sit-down dinners. We love it with lamb; try lamb kebabs on the grill, a good steak, or even char-grilled chicken.

If You Like Shiraz and Syrah

You're classy yet laid-back, elegant with a dash of anything-goes. Go a shade lighter and try a fruitier, less complicated Beaujolais Nouveau. Or, if you're a fan of dark, juicy fruit, go for a yummy, jammy Zinfandel.

What to Wear?

Shiraz's spicy-fruitiness demands an outfit with attitude—but go ahead and keep it casual, since Shiraz certainly isn't fussy! Try a quirky, colorful baby tee with a funky logo and a pair of low-rise gray and black striped pants. It's a fab outfit for Fridays at work, and it'll take you right to the BBQ or the bar afterward.

Zinfandel

Ladies, banish those college memories of drinking white Zinfandel from the bottle—white Zin that was so cheap, you could practically buy it with the change you fished out of the sofa cushions. (Ah, the good old days.) We're talking about *real* Zinfandel here, the red kind. It's a grape that yields wines that are often called "brambly," and "jammy," which means they serve up huge amounts of blueberry, blackberry, and even raspberry flavors. This delicious, darkly fruity wine bears no resemblance at all to that sickly sweet pink stuff we swilled when we were barely old enough to drink.

Zinfandel is a serious grape that knows how to have fun. We've never, ever heard anyone say, "Take that awful Zinfandel away from me!" so feel free to bust out a couple bottles anytime red or dark meat is involved (or chicken or fish, but only if it's seriously char-grilled). There's no wrong time to enjoy Zin. Try it with a drumstick from the Thanksgiving turkey, with burgers or ribs from the grill, or with a blackened chicken sandwich any time of year. Or try it on its own instead of a cocktail before dinner, or on a lazy, summery Saturday afternoon.

Zin's history is something of a twisty mystery. First of all, no one knows exactly where its name comes from. We know that Zin is very similar—although not identical—to the Primitivo grape in Italy, but its roots (no pun intended) trace to Croatia, and even earlier, to Greece or China. That makes it one supercosmopolitan grape! But today, it's regarded as "America's grape," and the top source for Zinfandel wines is California, including Sonoma and Napa Valleys.

If You Like Zinfandel

If you're a Zin drinker then you're into juicy dark fruit. Try a Pinot or even a Cabernet from California. You'll get plenty of that dark-berry flavor you love in the form of rich black cherries and blackberries!

What to Wear?

When you're drinking Zinfandel, you're obviously in the mood for a good time. Maybe you're having the girls over to share a bottle or two before going dancing! Tie on a bright red halter top, pair it with a short denim skirt, pour yourself a glass of Zin, and get the party started!

Gamay

You might have never heard of the Gamay grape, but chances are you've drunk a wine made from it. In late November, right before Thanksgiving, you might've seen signs in your local wine shop to the effect of, "Beaujolais Nouveau is here!" In that case, you're more familiar with Gamay than you thought. Beaujolais Nouveau is made from the Gamay grape grown in the French region of Beaujolais.

Beaujolais Nouveau (boh-zhuh-LAY nuh-VOH) is by far the most famous of the Beaujolais wines. Literally "new Beaujolais," it's the newest, most recent vintage of Beaujolais, and it's imported from France in massive amounts every November. Beaujolais Nouveau is a very, very young wine, and it's not the sort that improves with age, so you should drink it within just a couple months at most.

But that won't be hard! The one word that best describes Beaujolais Nouveau is *fun*, and that's because it's simply fruity, light, wonderful when gently chilled, inexpensive, and one of the most drinkable reds around. (Which means it's easy to polish off a bottle fairly quickly, so watch out!) You'll probably end up drinking it during the holidays, because it's available only in November, and that's fine. Lots of folks love it with turkey and sweet, heavy sides such as candied yams, stuffing, and even Aunt Edna's green bean casserole. Megan would rather share her stash with just a few guests at a holiday cocktail party, with lighter appetizers and hors d'oeuvres. However, she prefers something a bit more intense with sumptuous Turkey Day fare, like a hearty Cab. (Keep in mind, if you're like Megan, who adores a wine with a more sultry, smoky, spicy character, you'll probably want to skip the Beaujolais Nouveau.)

Top 5 Fab Reasons to Drink Red Wine

1. It warms you up on a cold day.
2. Studies show that the tannins in red wine are good for your heart!
3. You love yummy-but-heavy red meats like steak, cheeseburgers, and bacon.
4. Some red wines stain your lips so much you don't even need lipstick!
5. Your date brought over a bottle—and that's not all he's willing to share!

Spend a few more bucks on a cru (pronounced "crew") Beaujolais, which is Beaujolais from one of ten tiny towns or villages, or *crus,* in France. Cru wines are more complex, and you don't have to drink them right away. You can even hold onto good versions for a couple of years, if you want. A nice cru Beaujolais will run you about $15 to $20—a decent value, and a great gift for just about any wine drinker (especially yourself!).

If You Like Gamay Beaujolais

If you're a Gamay Beaujolais drinker you're probably looking for two things in a red wine: lots of refreshing fruit flavor and ultralight body. Go for a Shiraz from the United States or Australia if you're craving that bright fruit. Or choose a Pinot if you want a lighter wine that still has intense woodsy or smoky scents and flavors. (Blaufränkisch, anyone?)

What to Wear?

You drink Beaujolais Nouveau as soon as you buy it (remember, it doesn't age well), so that means it's the holiday season, because Beaujolais Nouveau is imported only in November. Tons of parties are thrown this time of year, so go clothes shopping for something festive and fun—just like Beaujolais! A snug, red velvet top over faded jeans is seductive and relaxed at the same time.

But if you're at a company holiday party, go with a little black dress and kitten heels, and invest in a shiny red clutch—that's the holiday spirit sans red-and-green cheesiness!

Sangiovese

Ah, Italia! Haven't we all dreamed of fleeing from our lives and taking off to Italy's Tuscany—land of sunshine, incredible food, and equally incredible wine? Well, it's a lot cheaper to buy a bottle of Chianti, some top-notch olive oil, and just pretend! Made from the Sangiovese grape, Chianti—which, as we all know, Hannibal Lecter likes to enjoy with fava beans and some unmentionable cuts of meat—has been around for hundreds of years, and its home is lush, sunny Tuscany.

Historically, wine buyers thought it was hard to find a decent Chianti, and poor Chianti's suffered a reputation as, well, a cheap, rather crappy red. But nothing could be farther from the truth! Italy's becoming a serious contender in the world of wine—after not being taken seriously by wine snobs for quite a long time—and today, there are lots of good Chiantis around. The really good ones are medium- or full-bodied, earthy and spicy, and even plum-y, made mostly from the Sangiovese grape blended with a little bit of other grapes, such as Cabernet or Merlot. Lighter, often less expensive versions often smell and taste like fresh cherries. Delish!

For everyday drinking, there's nothing wrong with just about any Chianti in the $5 range. (These are usually lighter in body.) If you find your five-buck bottle a bit rough, pair it with food and it'll shape right up. (Food improves any wine!) For special occasions—you just got a raise, you're having your boss over for dinner, or you just feel like a rock star—kick it up a notch and spring for a Chianti Classico, a slightly pricier version that will cost you about $15. The extra cash will, in this case, ensure that you get a more refined wine, more intense and earthy, sometimes peppery—and you won't get stuck with a lemon.

Chianti, not surprisingly, goes wonderfully with traditional Italian food. Pour a glass to accompany anything with red sauce such as pasta puttanesca, or pizza with fresh mozzarella, or bruschetta with basil, fresh tomato, and garlic. Or try it with lamb prepared with garlic and rosemary.

If You Like Chianti

If you like Classico Chianti you're into intense and earthy, so try a Cabernet from Chile. If a lighter Chianti rings your bell, you're probably a fan of the fresh red strawberry and cherry tastes, so try a Beaujolais Nouveau (in season, of course!) or a Zinfandel from California.

What to Wear?

If you've a hankering for a glass of Chianti, you're thinking of sitting at an outdoor café, sharing pasta with your sweetie à la *Lady and the Tramp.* Slip on a retro-style strapless dress with a flared, fluffy skirt and a sash at the waist. (Megan's roommate has one with a fun twin-cherry print!) You'll look sexy and spring-y at the same time.

Red Wines and Grapes You Don't Hear about All the Time—but You Should

Merlot, Cabernet, Pinot, Shiraz, Zinfandel, Sangiovese: They're responsible for some of the most popular red wines in the world—and with good reason! But these aren't the only red wines around. Just like your mom told you, there are other fish in the sea. And the other fish are darn good! Read on, and you'll learn about some up-and-coming reds and the grapes that make 'em. Oh, and coincidentally, these wines happen to be some of the best values around. We'll drink to that!

Tempranillo from Spain

Okay, ladies, there's one big problem with wines made from the Tempranillo grape: They're *too good* a value. Wines this delicious at this price have caused Megan and her roommate, Karen, to spend hours in wine bars, packing away way too many appetizers and not one but *two* bottles of vino. Whew. Tempranillo (tem-prah-NEE-yo) is the base of most Spanish wines, the most famous being Rioja from the Rioja region of Spain. Another famous region of Tempranillo production is the Ribera del Duero. Tempranillo-based wines can be fruity and spicy or rich, earthy, even chocolaty. And the prices are so right: It's easy to get a great wine in the $8 to $12 range.

What should you serve with Tempranillo wines? Besides just about anything, if you can get your hands on a hard Spanish cheese called Manchego, you'll have a match made in heaven. (Pairing wines and cheeses from the same country or region is never a bad idea!) Or bring it to a Labor Day cookout, and sip it alongside a grilled steak or pork chops. *Muy bien!* If you're vegetarian, take heart. Megan recently paired a Rioja with a "pizza" made from whole-grain flatbread, hummus, and cucumbers, and the combination was surprisingly good.

Try Tempranillo if you like smooth, easy-to-drink Merlot.

Valpolicella from Italy

Poor Valpolicella. Historically, it's been known as a pretty scrubby wine. No, you didn't want its number. No, you didn't want to give it yours. And no, you didn't want none of its time. But today, Valpolicella (vahl-pohl-ee-CHEL-la) is redeeming itself with the help of young Italian winemakers (many are women in their late twenties and early thirties!) determined to make it a world-class wine.

Valpolicella is a blend of four different grapes: Corvina, Rondinella, Molinara, and Negrara. It's inexpensive, good-natured, and delicious with hearty, everyday Italian fare. Look for "Valpolicella Classico" on the label for the best quality; but honestly, a decent Valpol that's fine for cracking open while you're sautéing the garlic should run you only about $10 at the most. We like it with things that are red or purple, including anything in rich tomato sauces, sausage pizza, and anything having to do with eggplant, like rollatini or caponata.

Try Valpolicella if you like a bright Chianti.

Malbec from Argentina

Megan cornered a cute-but-hapless bartender at Punch and Judy, a Manhattan wine bar. Right after Megan demanded to know if the climate in Lebanon was at all conducive to growing grapes (it is), she started in on him with a barrage of questions about Malbec. Is it originally from France? Who brought it to Argentina, its second home? And why? The poor

Make Your Own Wine Charms

Ever picked up a glass of wine (or beer, for that matter!) at a party, held it up, and asked, "Is this mine?"

Well, you no longer have to analyze lipstick stains to figure out if a wineglass is yours. Loop a wine charm around the stem of your glass so it rests on the base, and you'll recognize your glass in a crowd—and so can your guests if you give them a different charm for each of their glasses.

Wine charms can be as simple as tiny charms threaded around simple silver hoops, or as ornate and complex as tiny beads looped in intricate patterns. When we made a set, we went for the girly look, and used some small, simple pale pink and dark gray beads we found at a craft shop. And instead of spending extra money on pricier beads or metal charms, we spiced up our hoops with tiny pendants from some necklaces and earrings that we haven't worn in years. (It's amazing: You'd never wear that piece of costume jewelry again, but the little heart- or star-shaped pendant looks great when it's reincarnated as part of a wine charm!)

Here's how to make those fun little accoutrements called wine charms.

... *continued*

Materials

6–12 plain silver or gold earring hoops, 1 to 1¼ inch in diameter, available at most craft or bead stores

Beads; the size and colors are up to you. If you're going for the very small, delicate ones, be sure the hoop is thin enough to thread them on it. Not sure? Ask the store salesperson for help.

A bunch of costume jewelry you won't miss. Look for necklaces, earrings, and bracelets with small dangly charms or pendants that can easily be clipped from the chains.

Wire cutters

Instructions

1. Using the wire cutters, clip a few charms from the old costume jewelry. Use one to two charms per hoop (or more if you like, but we think it looks nicer if you don't go overboard).

2. Thread the charms and beads onto the hoops, alternating the charms with rows of beads in whatever pattern you like.

3. Leave a bit of space at the end of the hoop, so the beads don't go flying off when you open and close the hoop. And, of course, remember to use different charms or patterns on each.

Voila! Next time you're having a little shindig, attach one to each guest's wineglass. Wine charms add a little bit of style and sass—and you'll know exactly whose glass is whose. We'll toast to that!

bartender wiped his hands on a towel, said, "This is going to take me awhile," then did his best. In any event Megan learned that, yes, Malbec (MAHL-beck) is indigenous to the Bordeaux region of France, but is taking over the Argentinean wine world in a way that's even bigger than Mary-Kate and Ashley Olsen—and much less scary. Today, Malbec is flourishing like mad at the foot of the Andes Mountains, and like Tempranillo, Malbecs represent some of the best wine values out there. Affordable Malbecs smack of dark cherries and cinnamon spice. It's a juicy, erotic wine.

Treat yourself to a glass of Malbec with spicy chicken dishes (especially dark meat), any kind of red meat on the grill, bacon-wrapped dates (see page 64 for the recipe!) and hard cheeses.

Try Malbec if you like a jaunty, spicy Shiraz.

What's Hot Now?

What's red-hot in the wide world of red wines? Lots! Read on to find out which great French reds will never lead you astray; what to decant with Spanish tapas, the latest craze; why Portuguese reds are one of the best buys around; and lots more. Winemakers around the world are revving up their reds, and the good news is, it's easy to find Louis Vuitton quality at street-vendor prices. Get ready to paint the town red!

Italy

For absolutely no reason at all as far as we can see except snootiness, Italy hasn't been a major contender in the wine arena in the past. It was once renowned for second-rate Chiantis only good for tossing back with red sauce. But all that is changing now, and we have a bunch of young winemakers to thank for it. They're rejuvenating good ol' Valpolicella from old-running-shoe status to Manolo status, and have even created a new version called Valpolicella Superiore. And there are lots of fresh new Chianti Classicos on the scene that are great values. Keep your peepers peeled for a wine called Salice Salentino—a blend of Negroamaro (which literally means "black and bitter," but don't be alarmed!) and Malvasia. Salice Salentino tastes like cherries and leather—in the best possible way—and we've tasted versions for about $12 that just make us sigh in pleasure.

France

First things first. Here's a little caveat—and wine snobs across the country are going to gasp in horror when they hear this—if you're new to the charms of vino, France is probably not the best place for you to start. Once upon a time, when it came to wine, France was considered to be the alpha male, the big kahuna, the One and Only Big Cheese. And it still is a very large cheese. Just not the one and only. Nearly every country in the world is producing wine of all kinds today, so why limit yourself? Think of it this way: Say you're starting that exciting new job you've been angling for months. You decide it's time for a major wardrobe overhaul, and you head out on a shopping expedition in search of clothes worthy of your new position as Queen of the World. Would you head straight to Bendel's

AUSTIN

Looking for vino in **Austin?** Check out:

Fleming's Prime Steakhouse and Wine Bar (320 East 2nd St., ☎512-457-1500). Over 100 wines by the glass! It even features wine from Texas wineries.

Austin Land and Cattle Company (1205 N. Lamar Blvd., ☎512-472-1813), another classic, top-of-the-line Texas steakhouse with a well-balanced yet predominantly American wine list. Bottles are very reasonably priced. No matter what you're looking for, you'll find it at $25 to $30.

Malaga Tapas and Bar (208 West 4th St., ☎512-236-8020). You'll find literally hundreds of wines here, by glass and bottle. Why not try a flight (that's current lingo for a sampling) of wine? You'll get a few 2-ounce glasses, so you can taste different types of vino to your heart's content.

to buy an Armani suit if you were surrounded by dozens of fun, adorable boutiques and shops with windows full of the hottest new looks—many for less cash? Of course not.

This is not to say that all French wines cost a lot of money, or that France does not produce good wines (it does!). We're simply suggesting that, if you're a vino virgin, don't spend a lot of time worrying that you can't remember what the ten cru Beaujolais are or which wine districts of the Bordeaux region belong to the Left or Right Banks.

Instead, try as many different wines from as many different countries as you can. It'll only help you find out what you like.

And, of course, it's tough to answer the question, What's hot in France? Because the answer is always, Everything. Wines from the Rhône region are some of our favorites, and if you know where to look, you can find some first-class, red-hot, nutcracking bargains. From the northern slopes of the Rhône Valley, look for wines from Crozes-Hermitage (CROWS-AIR-mee-TAZH), where you'll find stellar Syrah-based wines. We've had some that actually smell like chocolate and breakfast pastries! From the southern side of the Rhône, look for the name Gigondas. Wines from this area taste a hell of a lot like those from the famed Châteauneuf-du-Pape, but cost less. Megan is just about addicted to wines that smell like leather, earth, and mushroom; if you agree, nab one from Gigondas! Be forewarned, though: Many of these wines cost around $20, so save 'em for special occasions, like your boss's birthday, or dinner with your boyfriend's parents. Looking for something cheaper? When in doubt, grab a bottle of under-$10 Côtes du Rhône from the southern Rhône. Chances are—although every producer is different—it'll be spicy, fruity, and easy drinking.

Spain

One word: Tempranillo. Go ahead and jump on the bandwagon. It's worth it! A huge number of Spain's wines are based on it. You'll find lots of bargains among them, and they're great to pair with traditional Spanish eats such as chorizo sausage and paella. We just had a Crianza Rioja that smelled and tasted like chocolate. Other wines from the Rioja region will remind you of strawberries and will smell like spices. And you may not have heard of the grape Monastrell, but it certainly has a presence in hot Spanish restaurants in Manhattan. It might be hard to find in your local wine shop, but keep an eye out for it the next time you're having tapas!

Portugal

You've already learned there's a lot more to Portuguese wines than just port. Red Portuguese table wines are little known in the United States, but they're quickly gaining in both popularity and quality. And there are tons of outstanding bottles to be had for around $10 to $15 or even less.

Portugal is packed with literally hundreds of grape varieties you can't find anywhere else in the world. There are so many, it's hard to keep track. In fact, in the past there were so many grapes that many winemakers didn't even know how many varieties were growing in their vineyards! Today, with modern science (and a lot of modern scientists who like wine), DNA testing is helping to figure all that out. It's still very tough for American buyers to tell what the heck a wine will taste like. That can be confusing, but it's also an adventure! Here's one hint, though: If you like Tempranillo from Spain, look out for the name "Aragones" on Portuguese wine labels because it's the same grape. Rising-star areas of Portugal include the Dão, Douro, and Alentejo regions. Never fear: Just like with wine from its neighbor, Spain, it's hard to go wrong with just about anything in the $7 to $15 region.

United States

When it comes to reds, look west, young woman! While red wines are produced all over the country, the Pacific Northwest is a foolproof source for some great ones, especially Pinot Noirs. And of course, California is still tossing out reds of all sorts, particularly Zins, left and right.

California

It'd be easy to write a whole book or five on California's wine industry and its up-and-coming wines! Suffice it to say that Napa Valley is still cranking out a lot of good Zinfandel. That's certainly no newsflash, but Cally Zins are often steady, well-priced winners. Petite Syrah, a bit of a sleeper, is making a comeback. Megan has had some fabulous Petite Syrahs from the Paso Robles and San Luis Obispo areas. One particularly wonderful wine smelled like earth and mint and blackberries and spice, and tasted like blueberries. Petit Syrah (little Syrah) hasn't gotten a lot of

. . . .

Hangover Cure #23

Want to guarantee you'll feel like a doormat in the morning? Stay out as late as possible, consume several bottles of wine by yourself, and then go to bed tipsy. Okay, we're being a bit sarcastic, but our point is, if the room is still spinning, don't go to bed! Stay up until you're feeling a little more steady, and while you're at it, do your best to drink tons of water and have a snack—preferably a mix of carbs, fat, and protein. (Our editor swears by peanut butter toast or cheesy scrambled eggs.) You might get slightly less sleep this way, but quality is always more important than quantity!

press, but wines made from it are intense, sensual—and we think they go right to your head!

Oregon

Think Pinot, and when you think Pinot, think Oregon's Willamette Valley, which is *the* best region for the stuff. If you find yourself stumped at the wine shop and you've got to have something red and delicious five minutes ago, grab a Pinot from Oregon. It's a no-fool plan.

South Africa

If you're looking for Cabs at really reasonable prices, look for selections from South Africa. We recently had one that smelled like blueberries and tasted like raspberries and chocolate—and went swimmingly with gamy things like venison and even lamb. Yum! And be sure to look out for Pinotage (pee-noh-TAZH), especially from the Stellenbosch region, which is priced between $7 and $14. Pinotage is a cross between the Pinot Noir and Cinsault grapes. It's spicy and jammy, and reminds us a bit of port wine. Very alluring!

South America

South American wines—from Argentina and Chile especially—are some of the best, class-A, red-alert bargains you'll find. And that's not because they're lacking in quality! We think it's extremely cool that many grapes made famous by France, such as Malbec, Cabernet, and the underrated Carmenere, are popping up in South America. Old-World wines with a brand-new twist!

Argentina

Argentina's the fifth-largest wine-producing country in the world, and the word on the street is, and has been, the grape Malbec. And with good reason. The stuff is doing just spiffily in Argentina—even better than it did in France—and tons of great wines are being produced at bargain-basement prices. Lots of good values can be found in the Mendoza and Maipú regions.

Chile

We're about to make a terrible joke: Chile is hot! (Okay, that was truly awful.) Chilean Merlots are clocking in at very low prices, and they're great examples of the stuff. Many taste like blackberries and other dark fruit and are supersmooth going down (and, we think, a lot less boring than many we've tasted!). Look for mouthwatering Merlots for around $9 to $12 or so from the Maipo region. And keep your eye open for Carmenere—especially in the Colchagua Valley region, which produces wines that are soft and smooth with sweet, tantalizing black fruit, black pepper, cassis, and cinnamon—kind of like Merlot combined with Zinfandel. Chile's also busting out with a bit of Syrah—it's not as cheap as Merlot, but worth the money if you can grab some.

Australia

For a long time, the Land Down Under was known almost exclusively for its Shiraz. And Australia still turns out some great Shiraz at prices so good they just about give you a heart attack. But now, Aussie's wine repertoire is expanding to include Pinot Noir (keep an eye out for the Pemberton region), Grenache, and Cabernets, to name a few. Hot, up-and-coming regions include Margaret River and Howard Park. Oh, and these days, winemakers all over Australia are combining Shiraz with a li'l touch of Viognier (a very fragrant, floral white grape) to make some blended wines that are a beautiful red-purple and have their own arresting fragrance. You won't see these every day, but if you can find one, they're worth the money!

New Zealand

Pinot Noir is taking over the world! Okay, maybe just New Zealand, but that's good enough for us. Australia and New Zealand have long been known for their Shiraz and Syrah, but these days the big thing is Pinot Noir. Of course, Pinot is and has been hot in the northwest United States, but New Zealand has only recently stepped up its production of Pinot.

Today, it's the most-grown grape in the country. And that's good for us! New Zealand's Pinots are big on cherry scent and flavor—a classic hallmark. Keep an eye out for anything from the Marlborough region. Syrahs and Cabs are also eternally popular here, and you can find some decent values under $15 with a little reconnaissance.

Germany and Austria

Neither Germany nor Austria are famous for their red wines! But that doesn't mean they don't have 'em. Most Americans just don't know about them. Although most famous for their whites, Germany and Austria both produce the red grapes Blaufränkisch (BLAW-fren-kish, rhymes with OW-frenkish) and Zweigelt (TSVEI-gehlt). They certainly haven't gotten a lot of press, but they're in all the hot restaurants, and they're pretty decent buys if you can snag them. Blaufränkisch smells like spice, tobacco, earth, and cherries, and it tastes like cherries, too. Zweigelt—one of Megan's faves!—can smell like mushrooms, spice, even a barnyard, and might taste like dried fruit. Try both in place of a Pinot Noir.

Get Ready to Paint the Town Red!

Maybe your new paramour's invited you for dinner at his house, and you want to let him know that you want to get, well, *cozy* later on. Or maybe your guy's parents are coming to dinner, and they're total oenophiles. Whatever! When it comes to red wines, you are so in the know. You've probably got a smoky bottle of Pinot on hand just waiting to be shared with someone sexy; or a great juicy Zinfandel just in case the girls stop by your place before hitting the bar on Saturday. And you're going to pick up a bottle of Valpolicella tomorrow because it goes perfectly with pizza. Whether you're looking to kick back with a book and a

You won't be stuck for a good bottle of vino in **Washington, D.C.,** as long as **The Wine Specialist** (2115 M St. NW, ☎202-833-0707) is around. While prices aren't dirt cheap, the selections are top-notch, and the über-knowledgeable sales staff is always eager to help.

glass of something red on a snowy winter night or relax outside on a breezy June evening, you know just which reds suit your mood! And most importantly, you know what you like. In fact, you're an expert on all wines *rosso*. Pour yourself a glass of your favorite red and celebrate!

Chapter Four

Pretty in Pink: Rosé Wines

Remember your college days? When you were so excited to turn twenty-one, you ran right for that $3 bottle of syrupy sweet pink wine that tasted like Hi-C gone wrong? Yeah, so do we. We've had so many bad experiences with pink wines (and wines that come in cardboard boxes), that we may well be traumatized for life. Recently, at a wine bar, Megan craved a glass of Riesling, but her brain short-circuited when she faced the hot bartender. She looked him in the eye and uttered words she'll never say again: "I'd like a glass of white Zinfandel, please." When the wine arrived, she screeched, "Why the hell is my wine *pink?*"

Good question. Pink wines—or rosé wines—get a bad rap. And, historically, this is for good reason. So many cheap, insipid, overly sweet versions clutter supermarket and liquor store shelves (depending on the liquor laws in your neck of the woods) that, if you don't know where to look, you'll end up with booze-flavored Crystal Light. But the good news is, there are diamonds in the rough! We'll show you where in the world to find delicious, reasonably priced rosé wines, what to serve with them, and why they're tons of fun. (Not that you'll need a lot of convincing.) And we'll even give you some tips for starting your own wine club as a fun way to try new varieties of vino, be they red, white, or pink. But every girl has a soft spot in her heart for pink wines, so embrace yours! Now's a good time to crack open a bottle of something pink and fruity, kick off your stilettos, and settle in for a bit. Relax: Everything's coming up roses!

So Why Is My Wine Pink?

Food coloring? Nope. (You could experiment with that if you want, but we don't recommend it!) The pink color comes from the skins of red grapes. The red skins macerate (soak) in the grape juice for just a few hours, not long enough to turn the wine fully red. It's like making a cup of tea. If you like your tea strong and dark, you let the teabag steep for a while. If you like your tea weak, you just dunk the teabag in the boiling water for a minute or two. Most rosés are not subjected to any kind of aging in oak. (Yay! This makes us very happy.) This means the majority of rosé wines are fresh, light, drinkable, and good with a wide variety of food. Think of rosés as happy mediums between reds and whites!

Top 5 Rosés Under (or Around!) $10

1. Xinomavro rosé from Greece
2. Kékfrankos rosé from Hungary
3. Grenache rosé from Spain
4. Anything Chilean
5. And, of course, anything from the south of France!

Rosés get a bad rap as low-quality soft drinks for grownups, but they sure as shootin' shouldn't! They may be pink, but they're certainly not "just weak red wines." These days, imbibers in the know take rosés more seriously. There's more to them than that $3 glass of white Zin! Oh, and if you're new to wine, rosés are a good place to start; they're so friendly, it's hard to dislike them. After all, who wouldn't like a fresh, zesty wine that's brimming with scents and flavors of strawberries, red cherries, red currants, raspberries, rhubarb, even watermelon, and other fun summer fruit? In some versions, you'll even find fascinating nuances of herbs and spices, such as white pepper. As it is with all wines, the nuances depend on the terroir in which the grape was grown, the winemaker's preferences, the weather that particular year, and other factors. What's the bright side of rosé's less-than-stellar reputation? Lots of rosés are reasonably priced, no matter where in the world they come from. So why not stock up?

What to Eat?

You can serve rosé with just about everything. That's the great thing about rosé wines. Lots of our friends like it particularly with chicken cooked just about any way you can imagine. A top-notch rosé with an oily fish like salmon really can't lead you astray. And it's also a treat with soft cheeses, particularly ones that aren't too stinky. Try rosés with turkey, pork, veal, salads of all sorts, savory brunch dishes like omelets or frittatas, and predinner nibbles like antipasti, mini quiches, and even clam dip (Hey, don't knock it till you've tried it!). You might even try rosé with the Thanksgiving turkey.

What to Wear?

Okay, how can drinking rosé wine *not* put you in the mood to wear something pink?! Come on; it's a great chance to embrace your girly side, even if you're the type of chick who wouldn't be caught dead in a skirt. Or if you're in a rush, toss on some bright pink metal bangles or quirky, oversized pink hoops, especially if you tend to stick with basic outfits in grays and blacks. It's a great way to dress 'em up without a lot of fuss!

Pouring and Storing the Pink

Rosés should be served slightly chilled at around 60 to 65 degrees. Feel free to use your all-purpose wineglasses, or, if you have them, white wineglasses. If you have leftovers (which we bet you won't!) pop the bottle in the fridge for up to three days after opening. White and rosé wines really shouldn't be put on ice or stuck in the freezer (it makes them too cold), but that's okay do in a pinch. It's better than drinking it warm!

When should you drink that rosé you just bought yesterday? How about right now? Rosés should be drunk right away, when they're as fresh as possible. Unlike some

Chill Out

Ever stuck a bottle of wine in the freezer for a few seconds to chill it quickly? So have we. To wine snobs, this practice is anathema, but it's very tempting if you picked up that bottle of rosé at the last minute and have to serve it ASAP! In a pinch, go ahead and do it. But be sure to keep an eye on it! Megan's friend Erin forgot she had popped a bottle of vino in the freezer, and left it there overnight. "The cork popped off," she said sadly, "and the wine was all iced over!" Then again, if someone gives you a really terrible bottle of wine, perhaps that'll make a good excuse: "Well, Lisa, I was just so excited to drink it I put it in the freezer—but then I got a phone call. It completely slipped my mind and in the morning the bottle was a wreck. I'm *so* disappointed!"

top-notch white and red wines, rosé won't benefit from aging. So don't put it in your cellar or on your wine rack and forget about it; drink it as soon as you can! We stick rosés in the fridge as soon as we buy them, to serve as a reminder every time we open the door.

What's Hot Around the World

Rosés from around the world are making strides in popularity! Gone is rosé's reputation as "so five minutes ago." Today, it's cutting edge! The great thing about rosé wines is, they're extremely versatile and go with a wide variety of food—and, of course, they're great all by themselves. They're refreshing and complex at the same time, no matter where in the world you find them!

Australia

It's true: The land of kangaroos and koalas is producing just about every type of wine under the sun these days—including rosés. Although rosés are not always easy to find in the States, they're plentiful in Australia. Look for examples from the Hunter Valley region. They might smell like strawberries or other sweet red fruit, and taste like cherries, raspberries, and other red fruit with a bit of a zing to them. Australian rosés are yummy with seafood of all sorts. We think they're especially fine with grilled shrimp. (Then again, we think everything is fine with grilled shrimp. Even chocolate ice cream.)

Chile

Known for its red wines, Chile's putting itself on the rosé map of the wine world. And, like many of the red wines, Chilean rosés are great bargains. No sickeningly

A Rosé by Any Other Year . . .

. . . would definitely not taste as sweet. Rosé wines are meant to be drunk young, young, young. So avoid any vintages older than two years. For example, if it's the year 2005 and you see bottles of 2002 vintage on the shelves, run, don't walk to the nearest 2004 vintage. Freshness is key!

Drunk in excess, any kind of wine will make you feel sick. Some tipplers think that rosés trigger a worse hangover than other wines. Perhaps that's because rosés usually are not bone-dry, or perhaps they're just so drinkable, another glass never sounds like it'll hurt. But you can have too much of a good thing, so make sure to split your drinking time between wine and water (or seltzer, or whatever your nonalcoholic poison may be). Rosé wines might go down smooth, but like any type of booze, it'll karate-kick you right in the liver if you overindulge.

sweet stuff here; expect them to be crisp and juicy. Good examples clock in at around $10.

Greece

It's not always easy to find Greek wines, but if you can, you'll be rewarded with some really reasonably priced rosés. Try one made from Xinomavro, one of Greece's oldest and well-respected grapes. It'll run about $14, or a few bucks less. Dry and crisp, it goes down dangerously smoothly and is great with lunch fare such as grilled chicken sandwiches, Cobb salads, and, of course, Greek appetizers of all sorts.

Hot Rosés from Hungary

Talk about bargains! Most people don't think of Hungary as the cutting edge of the wine world, but Hungarian wines are gaining more and more respect these days. Try a rosé made from the Kékfrankos grape (that's Greek for Blaufränkisch!) Salmon colored and fragrant, you'll get loads of that deep rich red fruit, and the one we tasted even smelled a bit like flowers. Try it with Greek or Middle

---

☙ LOS ANGELES ❧

Tippling in the City of Angels? When you're in **Los Angeles,** you need to check out:

A16 (2355 Chestnut St., ☎415-771-2216), where you'll find lots of interesting Italian wines by the glass and carafe (including Falanghina, Megan's favorite!) Plus, it's quite a scene after the sun goes down.

Bubble Lounge (714 Montgomery St., ☎415-434-4204) if sparkling wine is your thing. You'll be greeted by over 300 sparklers by the glass or bottle—plus a dance floor.

London Wine Bar (415 Sansome St., ☎415-788-4811) for something a little more laidback. It combines a friendly pub atmosphere with an extensive wine cellar—and knowledgeable, happy-to-help bartenders.

Eastern nibbles like hummus, tabbouleh, or spanakopita (spinach pie).

France

Fashions come and fashions go, but the French have been drinking rosés forever, especially in the south of France. They never go out of style! And you'll see a good number of French rosés in the $15 range (perhaps a little more, but they're definitely worth the extra francs, especially if it's a special occasion). If the only rosé wine you've ever had is the cheapest Californian stuff you can find, give a French version a go! With raspberry, red currant, and red cherry flavors, on the whole French rosés are light, juicy, and crisp. Just what a rosé should be. And they're good with light French fare like salads—especially salade niçoise—omelets, or a simple meal of Brie, crusty bread, and fresh fruit. Often made from the Cinsault grape, French rosés are particularly good wines for brunch.

Hot Rosés from Spain

When it comes to Spanish rosés, bargains abound! Looks for delish examples from the Rioja region of Spain for $15 and under. We like these with chicken, turkey, pork, and even cold roast beef sandwiches (spice fiends should skip the horseradish, though). Next time you and the girls are out for tapas, order a Spanish rosé instead of sticking to a basic red.

Start Your Own Wine Club!

All you need is a bottle, and a dream. But seriously, girls, starting a wine club is a fun way to feed your excitement over the fruit of the vine, and it's always a good excuse to get together with pals and let the spirit flow, so to speak. Plus, you'll save money and get to try tons of new wines, without cracking your piggy bank in two. Here's how:

● **Grab the girls (and the guys!).** Gather a bunch of buds who love wine as much as you do, and get them onboard for a monthly tasting. Reserve, say, the last Friday of every month, and ask a different wine lover to host each month. Having a core group of imbibers is cool, but encourage everyone to bring friends. As always, the more the merrier!

● **Choose your poison.** Pick a different theme each month, and base it on either a type of wine or a country. For example, in January celebrate Sauvignon Blanc and include examples from as many countries as possible, such as New Zealand, France, Australia, and Italy. In February focus on the wines of Spain with a Cava, a Spanish rosé, an Albariño, and a great red from Rioja. Ask each person to bring one bottle, and maybe something to snack on.

● **Serve good eats!** Where there's smoke, there's fire; where there's wine, there should always be food! You know that wine and food are a natural match—plus, you don't want anyone to end up with lampshades on their heads, or, more realistically, out on the front step in a wine-induced haze belting out "Mercedes Benz" by Janis Joplin. (Not that we'd ever do such a thing.) Bring cheese! Not only is it the perfect companion to wine, it requires no cooking, which is always convenient if you're in a rush. Some good standbys are Vermont Cheddar, aged Gouda, Manchego, ricotta

Searching for a place to buy wine in **Boston?** Head straight to **Best Cellars** (745 Boylston St., ☎617-266-2900, *www.bestcellars. com*; other locations nationwide), where the wines are labeled by taste: "fresh," "juicy," "big," or "sweet," to name a few. You don't have to remember complicated names or regions; you just have to know what you feel like drinking! And the best part is, none of the wines are bank breakers because many selections are $10 or less.

salata, Parmigiano-Reggiano, and blue cheese (Gorgonzola or bleu d'Auvergne, for example). We like to visit cheese shops for their price and selection, but you can probably find any of these at your local supermarket. Add some fresh fruit and bread, and you're good to go!

● **Take notes.** Write down the name of each wine, how it looks, tastes, and smells, whether or not you like it, and what foods match it well. Don't cheat! It's easy to say, "Oh, I'll just remember it," but in the morning you'll wake up wondering, "What the heck did I *drink?*"

● **Have fun!** And don't forget to keep an open mind. You're a woman of the world! Try everything, even if you suspect you won't like something. If you're not a fan, you don't have to finish the whole glass.

If you live in a large city, check out trendy wine stores. Many are starting to cater to wine clubs by recommending wines to try and supplying literature that gives you fun and savvy tips on what you're drinking. You might also want to consider taking field trips. Visit a local winery (they're not just in California—they're in New York, Michigan, Wisconsin, and many states in between) or check out a hip wine bar. Take a class at a wine or culinary school. Mix it up and have fun!

Think Pink

Some folks look at pink wine and say, "Why drink it?" We look at pink wine and say, "Why not?" Rosé wines are finally getting their due—very slowly, but very surely. They're fabulous with food, they're priced to drink tonight, and let's face it—they're tons of fun! By now you're probably on your way to the wine shop to stock up. Good going, Downtown Girl!

When can you drink rosé wines? Well, they're so flexible, the answer is, all the time. If your dinner party is split between die-hard red and white wine fanatics, get them to compromise with a Xinomavro from Greece. If you're having a tapas fiesta at your casa, invest in a couple of Spanish rosés and watch them disappear in minutes—along with those addictive bacon-wrapped dates! (See page 64 for the recipe.) Having brunch with buds? Bring over a bottle of something French and pink, and add some color to the afternoon.

✺ PHILADELPHIA ✺

Make a special trip to the City of Brotherly Love just to try some of **Philadelphia**'s great vinocentric bars!

Visit **Tank** (261 S. 21st St., ☎215-546-4232), where the prices are stellar. It's an excellent place to try wines that would ordinarily be too pricey.

Take your honey to **Davio's** (111 S. 17th St., ☎215-563-4810), a northern Italian steakhouse with an out-of-the-world wine list that's especially strong in selections from Italy and California.

Pink wines are so lovely to look at, and so easy to drink, they're just the thing to kick off a bridal shower, bachelorette bash, or engagement party. Drink them at a girls' night in while you're dishing the dirt on your latest guys, or commiserating about those awful lads you met online who just didn't stack up in real life. Rosé wines toast to everything girly. May you think pink forever!

Chapter Five

Sparkling Wines: Celebration in a Bottle

When Megan began her first foray into the world of online dating, she exchanged quite a few e-mails with a guy who seemed friendly, thoughtful, down-to-earth, and witty. Plus, he said his friends called him the "Celebration King" in honor of his outstanding partying skills. "Perfect!" Megan thought. "He sounds like a blast! The Celebration King is the man for me." So she agreed to join him for coffee.

He picked her up, and they headed for a cozy coffee shop on Boylston Street in Boston. All was well until they got out of the car—and until he opened his mouth. Megan was devastated—the Celebration King turned out to be a *bore*. (Or maybe Megan was just too much woman for him.) In any event, they just didn't connect. It simply wasn't a match made in heaven. Or anywhere else.

But, girls, take heart. The real Celebration King isn't a man. It comes in a bottle with a cork, it'll never try to feel you up, and it's absolutely delicious. The Celebration King is sparkling wine—especially from the famed region of Champagne in France. Sparkling wines turn a boring old Tuesday into, well, a celebration, and an ordinary Saturday into an event to (try to) remember. Everyone loves the festive *pop* of a cork, seeing the fizziness so effervescent it's practically alive, and experiencing the way the bubbles cleanse your palate and refresh your spirit. It's truly a party in a bottle!

In this chapter, you'll learn the difference between sparkling wine and true Champagne; what the heck *brut* means (is that a men's cologne?); how to throw a decadent Champagne-and-chocolate party that your friends will never forget, and tons more. Pop open a bottle of something bubbly, and read on!

It Has Bubbles: Is It Champagne?

Good question. Lots of people refer to any sparkling wine as "Champagne." But that's kind of, well, *wrong.* All sparkling wines, including Champagne, have bubbles and come in bottles with wire wrappers holding the pressurized corks in place. And that's where the resemblance ends. True Champagnes are made in the Champagne (shahm-PAHN-yeh) region of France. Period. Regardless of which variety of grape goes into making the sparkling wine, the wine is called Champagne. (Remember how the French like to name their wines after the place the grape is grown, not the name of the grape? There you go.) Which means that a sparkler made from grapes grown in, say, upstate New York is not true Champagne (and probably won't taste remotely like Champagne, although it may be quite tasty). So, feel free to call Champagne by its place name if it's grown in

Girls and Grapes

One of the most famous women in vinous history, Madame Clicquot (of the House of Clicquot, famed makers of top-quality Champagne) is credited with an innovation in traditional Champagne-making called riddling. It's a process of collecting sediment in the neck of the bottles so the sediment can be removed easily. By inverting the bottles, gradually tipping them toward the vertical and rotating them every few days for six to eight weeks, the winemaker encourages the sediment to settle in the neck of the bottles. Once settled, the sediment is finally disgorged—that is, expelled from the neck of the bottle. The riddling process is now an indispensable part of Champagne making. After Madame Clicquot's husband died when she was just a twenty-something, she ran his eponymous winery and helped guide it to greatness. We'll pop open a bottle to that!

France, but do us a favor and refer to everything else as sparkling wine. Because that's what it is.

What is *not* Champagne? Well, do you remember those bottles of $3.99 pink "Champagne" you kicked back on your twenty-first birthday? (Or was that just us?) Don't slander the name of a heavenly beverage such as Champagne by tossing it into the same category as something with the word "Duck" on its label. If it wasn't made in the Champagne region of France, call it "sparkling wine." You'll sound like a true expert!

The only exceptions are sparklers made by a few wineries in the United States—only about five or six—who are legally permitted to sell their sparkling wine as Champagne anywhere in the world. These wineries were founded by Frenchmen, then "grandfathered" in, so to speak. (Megan visited one of these wineries in New Jersey, where she had an incredible blueberry Champagne—divine with brunch!)

Come quickly! I'm drinking stars!
—Dom Pérignon, the blind monk credited
with the invention of Champagne, to his assistant

So, if it's not from France and it calls itself Champagne, beware. If a sparkling wine has to ride on the coattails of Champagne to sell itself, that's not a very good sign. Champagne is and always has been the lord of the sparklers but great sparkling wines are made all over the world these days. There's no need for them to be called Champagne for them to taste good.

Is Champagne Made from "Champagne Grapes"?

No. Champagne is made from a blend of three grapes: Pinot Noir, Pinot Meunier (a lesser-known black grape), and Chardonnay. At a recent tasting, we got the chance to try a variety of Champagnes and cognac from a well-known Champagne producer. The man leading the tasting gave some rather, um, *interesting* answers to guests' questions, so we decided to feel him out by asking, "Pardon me, but we were wondering what grapes are used to make Champagne?"

MINNEAPOLIS

If you're looking for a location for a romantic tête-a-tête in **Minneapolis,** look no further than:

Bev's Wine Bar (250 3rd Ave. N., ☎612-337-0102), where simple and elegant appetizers meet a well-formed wine list; if the list seems daunting, your server will be more than happy to give you a bit of guidance.

Beaujo's Wine Bar and Bistro (4950 France Ave. S., ☎952-922-8974), a friendly, unpretentious, comfortable joint. Savor a bottle from the global wine selection with dinner.

He looked nervous for a split second, quickly recovered and said, "Champagne grapes, of course." Hmmm. Really? So is cognac made from cognac grapes? Vodka from vodka grapes? Peach schnapps from peach schnapps grapes?

So, ladies, those cute little bunches of grapes you see in stores called Champagne grapes are *not* the grapes used to make Champagne. They make fun decorations, but don't try to crush them in your bathtub in the hopes of making vintage Champagne!

Making the Stuff

How do the bubbles get into the bubbly in the first place? Well, there are a couple of different ways, and one is definitely better than the other. Look for the phrases *méthode traditionale, méthode champenoise, méthode ancestrale,* or "naturally fermented in this bottle" on the label of bubblies you're considering buying. Sparklers from locations outside France, such as Spain or Italy, might not indicate this on the front label, but turn the bottle around and check the back label. You can often find a brief description of the wine and the winemaking process there. All sparklers undergo two fermentations. The first turns grape juice into a still (non-sparkling) wine, and the second turns the still wine into a bubbly. Sparklers made the traditional way undergo the second fermentation right in the bottle. It's a much more complex process involving longer aging, riddling (see page 131), and then *flash-freezing* the bottle's neck and expelling

Hangover Cure #681

Oh, no! You stayed out way too late last night, and that last glass of Rosé pushed you over the edge. And this morning, you're jumping on a plane—perhaps to head back to school, to your little sister's wedding, or to Florida with a bunch of gal pals. What to do? Quick! Assemble an Emergency Hangover Kit, so you'll be able to feel better on the go, and have plenty of supplies in case you're faced with another hangover on your travels! Pack bottled water to keep you hydrated, salty snacks to help your dehydrated body retain fluids (and besides, you need to eat), Diet Coke to give you a jolt of caffeine, gum or mints to ease cotton mouth, chocolate because you deserve a treat, aspirin for that headache, and a jump rope and running shoes because you should work up a good sweat at the first opportunity. Everything you need to feel like a new woman!

sediment like a funky ice cube. Cool, isn't it? (You'll laugh, you'll cry; it's better than *Cats*.) And all that work pays off. You'll inevitably get a better bubbly this way.

Sparklers can also be made (very fast, very inexpensively) through the bulk or Charmat (shahr-MAH) method, in which the second fermentation takes place in a huge metal tank instead of in each bottle. Skip 'em. These days you can find Champagnes and other sparklers from around the world made by the traditional method at very reasonable prices (as low as around $8 to $12). And you'll certainly be getting a better wine. We just had a great Spanish Cava made by the traditional method, which was only $6.99!

Budget-Busting Bubbly?

Champagne has a reputation for being very, very expensive, which is why it's traditionally saved for special occasions. And while real Champagne starts at $20 (and that's if you find a spectacular sale), other sparklers of all sorts are available for between $5 and $500. And, just as it is with still wines (that is, nonsparkling wines), spending more won't always get you a better bottle. Our goal is to point you in the direction of great sparklers from all over the world for under $20. Maybe it's your best friend's bachelorette party, your anniversary (and you plan on spending it alone with your sweetie in a dim, candlelit room!), or perhaps you finally, *finally* got that raise you were angling for. Whatever the occasion, there's a bubbly to fit your budget.

Vintage Champagne

Vintage Champagne is made of the best grapes from just one vintage. That makes it more expensive, because the weather that year was just right and the winemaker paid plenty of extra attention to her top-notch wines. She used only the best grapes and aged the Champagne considerably longer than its nonvintage counterparts. If the weather isn't great, chances are that Champagne houses won't produce a vintage Champagne that year. You'll probably pay around $75 for vintage Champagne. (We drink it only when a rich suitor is paying for it, during expense account business dinners, or when we've had a really, *really* bad week at work.)

As a styling Downtown Girl, you know that nothing gives an outfit a bit of pop like a some funky vintage accessories you picked up a for song at some little hidden boutique—or your grandmother's jewelry box. Vintage is elegant, funky, and affordable. Not so with vintage Champagnes! Here's where things get pricey. If you splurge on a

Size Does Matter

Bigger isn't always better—when it comes to bubbles, that is! The better a sparkler is, the smaller its bubbles will be. If your sparkler feels like seltzer water in your mouth, you've got a lemon. This doesn't indicate that the wine itself has gone bad; it just means you're probably drinking something pretty darn cheap. Try a variety of sparklers, from a decent Champagne to a $4 bottle of something pink and plastic-corked, and you'll see what we mean!

bottle of vintage Champagne—the words "vintage Champagne" will be clearly marked on the label—you really should save it for a special occasion! A tip for the tippler: Try a vintage Champagne after you've tried a good variety of less expensive Champagnes and other sparkling wines; you'll really notice the difference.

The Oh-Champagne-You're-So-Fine Print

Champagne has a mystique, no doubt about it. Is it the golden color? The way the bubbles delightfully tingle and tease the tip of your tongue? Maybe? It could also be the cryptic abbreviations you find on every bottle of bubbly. No worries! We'll help you decode it—in laywoman's terms.

A six-digit number appears on every Champagne label, preceded by two little letters. The numbers can usually be found in the lower right corner of the label, or along the label's right side. About 90 percent of the time, the two letters will be N.M. or R.M. Without getting too technical, "N.M." stands for "négociant-manipulant," and means that the producers and merchants don't own their own vineyards, but rather buy the grapes from other folks, and then turn the grapes into Champagne. Almost all the popular, best-known Champagnes are N.M.

"R.M." is an abbreviation for "récoltant-manipulant," referring to the independents who grow their own grapes, produce their own Champagnes, and sell 'em themselves. Here's where you'll find diamonds in the rough. Wines from these houses often cost a little more, and might be a little tougher to find, but they're worth it. Shopping for R.M. Champagne is the equivalent to shopping at a privately owned boutique in Soho instead of the Gap. You may have to shell out a little more cash, but chances are you won't spot some chick on the street wearing *your* skirt! Plus, it's likely that your $50 skirt from that boutique will be a better-made garment than its $40 counterpart at a chain store. Get it?

How Sweet It Is! (Um, How Sweet <u>Is</u> It?)

Brut? Is that men's cologne? Not when you're shopping for sparkling wine! Just like still wines, some sparklers are as dry as the Sahara, while others are dessert-caliber sweet. You'll see the following classifications most often on Champagne and French sparklers, but other sparklers from around the world sometimes use them, too, so that you, Ms. Consumer, will know (approximately) how sweet your sparkler will be. We've demystified the classifications for you, in plain English:

> *Demi-sec = really sweet, dessertlike*
> *Sec = sweet, but not quite as sweet as demi-sec*
> *Extra dry = a little sweet*
> *Brut = pretty darn dry*
> *Ultra or extra brut = as dry as you can get*

Most of the Champagnes you see in a wine shop or liquor store are extra dry or brut. For everyday drinking, and for pairing with food, stick with the extra dry, brut, and extra brut versions. Save the sweeter ones for dessert or to enjoy as an after-dinner drink.

Sparkling Wine in a Six-Pack?

Absolutely. Single-serving bottles of Champagne and sparking wine are the newest thing in cool. Forget those dreadful cocktails-in-a-can that lined the shelves of grocery stores twenty years ago. While single-serving bottles are not cheap—a pack of four can run you up to $40—they're lots of fun. Look for versions by Pommery winery (French) and Niebaum-Coppola (California) winery. Oh, and if you want to look über-trendy, be sure to sip them through a straw—just like the supermodels do so they won't muss their lipstick.

The Letters on the Labels

Does N.V. on the label stand for Nevada? Nope, not in this case. It stands for "nonvintage." Nonvintage Champagne is made from grapes from more than one harvest, or vintage. That means a bottle of N.V. Champagne could be made from grapes harvested in 1999, 2001, and 2002. Don't get your knickers in a knot. It's still great Champagne! N.V. Champagnes account for the vast majority of Champagnes on the market.

Thinking Pink?

You're not alone. Rosé sparklers and Champagnes, once denounced for being supersweet, cheaply made, and generally crappy, are back in vogue and being poured at the hottest parties around. And don't be fooled by the pretty color;

today's rosé Champagnes aren't syrupy and cloying. Made by adding red wine, usually Pinot Noir, to the blend (or, in some cases, allowing Pinot Noir skins to macerate [soak] in the base wine prior to any fermentation), these bubblies are dry wines, but they often have a dash of fresh fruit, especially strawberry, to their scents and flavors. It can be a bit tricky to find one under $20, but keep your eyes open. It's definitely something you'll want to share with the girls on a night in, to celebrate your best bud for finally dumping that jerk, to toast your acceptance to graduate school, or just to rejoice that it's a Friday! Rosé sparklers also make great gifts, and if you bring one to a party, you're sure to be a hit with your hosts.

The Fuzzy Bunny

If you're looking for a different twist on pink Champagne, try a Fuzzy Bunny; it's the perfect excuse to buy that cheap pink $3 sparkler you still get an odd craving for.

1 ounce vodka
½ ounce peach schnapps
4 ounces rosé sparkler or pink Champagne
5 or 6 jellybeans per glass

1. Pour vodka into a Champagne flute. Add peach schnapps, and then toss in the bubbly.

2. Drop a couple of jelly beans into the bottom of the glass. This potent little elixir will be a hit with everyone!

Serving the Bubbly

Like still white wine, sparkling wine should always be served chilled (but never ice cold—we're not slugging back lite beer here!). About half an hour in the fridge should cool it sufficiently. (Megan's been known to throw it in the freezer for a couple minutes, but only under great duress.) Should you put it in an ice bucket? The jury's out. Some say putting Champagne or sparklers on ice chills them too much and ruins their flavors; others make it a practice. We think you should just finish the bottle before it warms up!

As we mentioned earlier, skip those saucer-shaped glasses, the ones with the extra-wide mouths. They're pretty, sure, but the increased surface area de-bubbles the bubbly. And that's no good! Plus, we have a tough time drinking out of them without spilling the sparkly stuff all over ourselves.

Anyway, you should always use Champagne flutes. As the song goes, they're simply the best. If you're having a party, skip the Dixie cups and grab some plastic Champagne flutes from the grocery store. They're classier, and besides, you don't have to feel bad about throwing them away at the end of the night!

Opening the Bottle

Ooh, this is the fun part! Nothing says, "Let's party!" like the pop of a Champagne cork. So grab a bottle, and let it rip. No need to be nervous, ladies. Just make sure

Engagement Parties That Sparkle

People buy Champagne and sparking wine to celebrate nuptials more than any other event. If it's your job to plan the wedding shower or engagement party, serve Champagne and make it a Stock the Bar party! After all, what couple wouldn't love a gift of wine, barware, or other booze-related accessories? Keep it low-key and plan it for cocktail hour—around 6 P.M.—on a weekday night. Serve easy-to-make appetizers, such as bacon-wrapped dates and baked Brie (see pages 56 and 64 for the recipes) and plenty of drinks, and then have the bride and groom open gifts. It's no fun to watch them open gifts of bathroom towels and spatulas; it's *so* fun to watch them open gifts of funky stemware, and great wines! Good time guaranteed.

the thing has been resting in the fridge for a while, so it's nice and cool, and don't swing it over your head as though you're trying to lasso a wild mustang, and you'll be fine. First, remove the foil from the neck of the bottle. Untwist the wire cage with one hand while keeping the other hand on top of the bottle. Slip the cage off and toss it.

Now grab a cloth, and aim the bottle away from any immediate walls, people, small animals, and anything else you might not want to maim. Hold the bottle's neck with one hand, the cloth-covered cork with the other, and then twist the bottle gently till the cork pops loose. No explosions necessary!

Pouring the Bubbly

We like to tilt the flute when we pour sparkling wine, even though some say it ruins the mousse (the frothy head that foams to the top when you pour it). If you like being in control, you'll probably rather tilt the glass a touch than waste any of the bubbly fizzing over. Or, if you want to take a chance you can hold the bottle by the neck and pour *very slowly and carefully.* If you're really aiming to impress, you can place one thumb into the center of the arch at the bottom of the bottle (known as the "punt" in winespeak) and rest the palm and fingers of your other hand on the curve of the bottle. Gently pour into the flutes.

Bubbles and Nibbles

What to eat with Champagne and sparkling wines? Anything! (Well, almost anything.) Dry and relatively dry bubbly wines are great for cleansing your palate between courses. They're also delicious with fried foods, anything oily, appetizers such as antipasto or soft cheese with crackers, brunch foods such as omelets, salads, and other light meals or snacks. We love to enjoy a glass of Champagne with a simple handful of salty mixed nuts. (More on sparkling wines in What's Hot Around the World, page 145.)

Dress up a glass of any sparkling wine by dropping a fresh berry into the bottom of the glass after pouring. We like to use cranberries, raspberries, or blueberries. It's the easiest thing ever, and it adds an extra dash of color. Guaranteed to elicit oohs and aahs from your guests!

What to Wear?

What a conundrum! Champagne is versatile; it's elegant, simple, yet luxurious. (We want to be just like Champagne when we grow up!) It can dress up an early autumn picnic, or complement your little black dress perfectly at a world-class soiree. While it's fluid enough to suit your every mood, we love to sip a glass when we're in the mood to feel chic, sleek, and like queens of the world.

At her latest Champagne-and-chocolate party (see page 149 to learn how you can throw your own!), Megan debuted her all-time favorite, sample-sale find: a tight black asymmetrical top with a quirky red-and-silver beaded trim. Paired with black jeans and boots, it was the perfect glam-yet-cool companion to her flute of bubbly. Another idea is to wear anything gold—in honor of Champagne's golden hue. That doesn't mean dragging out the gold lame dress from your prom. Concentrate on little touches—gold Manolo Blahniks or gold bangles, particularly if they have diamond accents. Champagne's effervescence demands a little sparkle!

"I drink it when I'm happy and when I'm sad. Sometimes I drink it when I'm alone. When I have company, I consider it obligatory. I trifle with it if I'm not hungry and drink it when I am. Otherwise, I never touch it—unless I'm thirsty."

—Madame Lily Bollinger, who ran the celebrated Champagne house of that name from 1941 to 1977, in reply to the question, When do you drink Champagne?

What's Hot Around the World

Hold on to your hats—and your Champagne flutes! Champagne may be the grande dame in the world of sparklers, but that doesn't mean there aren't tons of top-notch bubblies from around the world—often at prices so low you'll think you're dreaming.

Italy, Land of the Stellar Sparkler!

Think fast. What can you serve with appetizers—especially Italian ones—that your guests are guaranteed to love? Prosecco, a lightly sparkling (or *frizzante*) wine from Italy's Veneto region. Made from the Prosecco grape, this wine often smacks of yellow or green apples, pears, even flowers. So light and refreshing, it will cleanse your palate and heighten your appetite. Good Prosecco runs about $9 to $11 per bottle, a less expensive yet in-the-know alternative to Champagne.

Another yummy Italian sparkler that'll brighten any shindig—especially brunch—is Moscato d'Asti, a wine made from the Muscat grape. Some think it's best as a dessert wine, but we think you can drink it with anything, because its honeyed, honeysuckle, and tangerine aromas and flavors make it delicious with any meal. Sip it on the weekends alongside light lunch fare, such as salads or omelets, or enjoy a glass by itself in late afternoon. And since it's very low in alcohol, you won't have to worry about feeling sleepy after a glass or two. It's great for bridal showers, as a kickoff to a bachelorette party, or for springtime brunches.

United States, Land of Plenty of Sparklers

American sparklers—they're not just for the Fourth of July anymore! No, these aren't the kind of sparklers you set on fire, then twirl around. They're delicious sparkling wines you'll love, and they're a great alternative to Champagne. Lots of wineries across the United States produce sparkling wines, but you'll find some particularly yummy ones from upstate New York, where the relatively cool climate is superconducive to making the bubbly. Good sparklers from upstate New York and the Finger Lakes region might not always be easy to find, but if you can put your hands on one, grab it. New York sparklers cost between $10 and $20, and they're worth every cent. And of course, California puts out tons of sparklers every year, including lots of good ones from Mendocino County and Sonoma County. Each wine is different, but lots of Cally-style sparklers smell and taste like ripe fruit (more fruity than their French counterparts) and freshly toasted bread. Prices vary wildly, but you'll be able to find some solid sparklers in the $15 to $20 range fairly easily.

France, Land That Invented It

The last word in wines of all kinds, France is tossing out some yummy sparklers that are a great alternative to pricey Champagnes. Again, when it comes to wine, what's *not* hot in France? It's the home of the famed Champagne region, but other regions of France are also producing top-notch bubblies, and at can't-be-beat prices! Look for examples from the Loire Valley for around $10, sometimes even a bit lower. And check the label for the word *crémant,* which means the wine was made by the traditional method, and that means you'll probably get a better wine.

Oh, and look out for peach-flavored sparkling wine from France. Lush and fruity and lightly sweet, Megan had it years ago—but now it seems to have disappeared from the shelves of her favorite wine shop. At under $10, it was a steal, and she misses it terribly. If you find it, let us know!

Spain, Land of the Dry Sparkler

Spanish sparklers represent great values—at these prices, you'll want to drink them every day! Called Cavas, sparkling wines from Spain tend to be desert-dry or off-dry, and, like Prosecco from Italy, they make great aperitifs. Try them before dinner with appetizers of all kinds. They're often yeasty or earthy, not fruity; perfect for folks who think sparkling wine is *always* sweet and refuse to drink it. And at around $7 a bottle—no kidding!—you'll be dying to turn Cava into sparkling sangria, pour it with lunch *and* dinner, or indulge in a sparkling nightcap as you curl up on the couch with a book. Oh, and look for rosé Cavas, too, to the tune of $10!

Australia, Land of Sparkling Shiraz

Because the Land Down Under is renowned for its Shiraz, it's no wonder Australia produces a *sparkling* Shiraz. Yes, you read right: a red sparkler. It certainly doesn't come cheap—we've seen examples between $16 and $32 per bottle. And it may take a little searching before you can put your hands on one. It's got Shiraz's signature fruitiness,

---

Sangria with a Twist

At your next party, skip the punch and make sparkling sangria instead! The bubbles add jazz to any bash.

1 apple	1 bottle Cava
1 orange	1 ounce triple sec
2 ounces vodka	Dash of lime juice

1. Slice one apple and one orange and toss them into a pitcher.
2. Add 2 ounces vodka. Then slowly pour a bottle of Cava over the fruit.
3. Add 1 ounce triple sec and a few dashes of lime juice, and taste. If it's too sweet, add more lime juice; if it's too tart, add more triple sec.
4. Stir gently, and serve in wineglasses or tumblers. Try it at brunch!

---

and it smells and tastes like dark fruit (plums, black cherries), and even chocolate. It's incredibly seductive, so we think it should be kept for special occasions—such as a Tuesday night when you and your guy are feeling particularly amorous!

You'll also see the occasional sparkling Pinot Noir, but these are even harder to find than sparkling Shiraz.

A Note on New Zealand: While sparklers from New Zealand probably won't be on the shelf of the liquor store on your corner (unless it's an in-the-know wine shop!), Kiwi sparklers are worth a go if you do come across one or two. New Zealand's cool maritime climate is conducive to producing good bubbly, so chances are you won't go wrong.

Throwing a Champagne-and-Chocolate Soiree

This shindig is always a huge hit, no matter how many people you invite, and, although it's definitely decadent and fun, it's absolutely no fuss. Okay, so technically it's tricky to pair Champagne and chocolate. In fact, wine snobs would turn up their haughty noses at us for suggesting it. But in this case, the point isn't the perfect matching of food and wine, it's about pure hedonism. After all, what could be more delectable than marrying two of the world's most sinful, made-for-celebration treats?

Invite as few as eight to ten people, or as many as forty. But beware: Megan held her first Champagne-and-chocolate party way back in college, and loads of people crashed the party, cramming into her tiny dorm room to join the festivities. When people you don't even know show up to a party, it's a testament to your reputation as the hottest hostess around!

Here's what to do:

● **Buy the bubbly.** You can figure about one drink per person per hour. Regular-size (750 ml) bottles of sparkling wine carry about four to six glasses. So if you're inviting ten people to a four-hour shindig, you'll want to get about eight to ten bottles. It's always better to have leftovers than to run out!

● **Serve your best or favorite sparklers first.** Why? Alcohol dulls the senses. Be sure to serve the best bubbly as soon as everyone arrives just in case the second or third glass goes to your head too fast!

● **Make sure you have other beverages on hand.** In case any of your guests aren't fans of sparkling wine, or if they choose not to drink, be sure to stock other alcoholic and nonalcoholic choices. We keep bottles of vodka, rum, triple sec, amaretto, and sour mix, as well as a variety of juices, on hand at all times. You never know when you'll need 'em!

● **Do serve more substantial food, not just chocolate.** Always a good rule of thumb, whenever you're serving alcohol to your guests! Lay out cheese, crackers, nuts, fruit, chips, dip, whatever you'd like. Just make sure you give potentially hungry guests something besides sweets to nosh on. Sparklers go especially well with salty food, light bites, and anything fried. Check out our recipes for easy baked Brie (page 56), and bacon-wrapped dates (page 64).

If you're planning a huge bash, why not ask friends to bring a bottle of Champagne or another sparkler, or something devilishly chocolaty—to share? That way, you won't have to spend quite as much, and everyone will be able to try lots of different wines. Our favorite part of being a hostess is introducing guests to one another and watching them make new friends and contacts. It's so much fun! Make as many introductions as possible. For weeks to come, everyone will be talking about what a good time they had at your party!

A Sparkling Personality

Our favorite thing about sparkling wines is, it's hard to find a truly terrible one. Even when you do, you still won't want to let it go to waste! There's something about bubbly wine—its headiness, its unique fragrances and flavors, its crispness on the tongue—that'll make you high on life. And there are so many great sparklers on the market at reasonable prices, that you can really treat yourself to a glass every day, any time of year.

Sparkling wines are for New Year's. They're for celebrations of the grandest order. But they're also for a weeknight when you're watching *Queer Eye*. They're for sipping on a gray, misty day on a rickety bench overlooking German vineyards. They're for toasting to new love under a tree by the Charles River. They're for sipping after company softball games, whether your team wins or loses. Sparkling wines are, truly, Celebration Kings.

Chapter Six

Dessert Wines: Port, Sherry, and More

S top. We know what you're thinking. "Port? *Sherry*? Gross. They're for old people or losers who don't know how to drink." Well, girls, hold on to your Kate Spade handbags: We're about to debunk that myth and change your lives in a few short pages—forever.

But wait! Don't feel bad. We used to think the same thing. After all, port and sherry—and dessert wines of all kinds— tend to suffer a bad rap among drinkers under the age of fifty. But as we tasted a few different selections and learned more about them, especially about the mysterious beverage port, we realized something revolutionary: Port is *sexy*. In fact, it may be the sexiest drink in the world. Its richness heats you up from the inside out and if you're not careful, you'll want to rip your man's clothes off after a glass or two. And if that's not reason enough to try it, we don't know what is!

Whew. We were getting carried away there! As we were saying, in general, dessert wines can be summed up in one word: *yum*. Sweet and fragrant, just a sniff of a good dessert wine will produce contented sighs. It's impossible *not* to fall in love with them! In this chapter, you'll learn how to serve the sweet stuff, what to eat with it, and lots more. Read on, and prepare to be seduced!

What Is Port?

It has nothing to do with being portly, nor is it produced in port cities across the world. (Although those are good guesses!) Its name comes from the city of Oporto, in Portugal (remember, real port comes from Portugal only). And, get this: Port is made from dozens and dozens of different grapes indigenous to Portugal. In fact, until not very long ago, vintners didn't necessarily know which grapes were growing in their own vineyards! So "real" port comes from Portugal only, although winemakers across the world are experimenting with their own versions of the stuff. We even tasted a delicious American version with blueberry extract added to it! Perhaps we shouldn't be so surprised—dark fruit like blueberries matches well with port's brooding spiciness.

Port is a fortified red wine, which means it has alcohol—in port's case, brandy—added to it. That's why port's alcohol content is high (which means it's not something you'll want to chug like cheap like beer!).

Port for the Single Girl

Stand in front of the port shelves at the liquor store or wine shop, and you might find yourself scratching your head. "Do I have to spend $50 for a good bottle of port? What's the difference between 'tawny' and 'ruby' types of port?" Never fear. Here's a little rundown of the main types of port—but of course, it's up to you to decide what you like!

Ruby Port

Ruby port is great way to give port a shot without parting with tons of cash. Aged only about two years in either wood or stainless steel, this type of port is meant to be drunk young. When you pour yourself a glass, take a good look at the color. It's beautiful, a deep ruby red (hence the name) bordering on garnet. It might smell like vanilla or black fruit, often blackberries. Ruby ports are usually medium-bodied and pretty high in tannin.

Again, a wine is high in tannin if you feel it "grip" your teeth.

Tawny Port

Yum! When you get a good tawny port, it's oh so good. Tawny's our favorite kind of port, and it's a little more expensive than ruby port, but so worth the extra bucks. Tawny ports are aged a bit longer than rubies, about six years or sometimes more, in wooden casks. You might notice that the price increases with the age. To get the best quality for the best value, go for the ten-year versions at about $25. They're usually a lovely brownish-red color. Our favorite tawnies smell and taste like nuts, toffee, and dried peaches. They're delicious along with a simple piece of shortbread!

Late-Bottled Vintage Port (or LBV Port)

Made from grapes harvested in the same year—unlike other ports, which can be made from grapes from several different vintages—LBV port is generally aged longer in wood (often oak) than ruby or tawny port, and it comes out supersmooth and ready to drink. (When Megan tried an LBV for the first time, it hit her: LBV port is an aphrodisiac!) It's a good alternative to vintage port (described next), partly because you don't have to wait decades to drink it.

Vintage Port

It's la crème de la crème, as they say. But there's a catch to vintage port—a catch or two, that is. First, the stuff is often way too pricey for our budgets. At $75 to $100 (or even a little more), we'd buy ourselves a bottle only if we won the lottery. Although, if you have to get someone a gift, we can't imagine anyone who wouldn't be thrilled to receive a bottle of vintage port—especially us! Also, when sold it has aged only a couple of years, so when you buy it, you won't be able to drink it for, quite literally, decades. If you do decide to go for broke—or, better yet, if someone gives you a bottle—you can expect vintage port to be rich, with aromas and flavors of deep black fruit.

The Skinny on Serving

Don't stick port in your liquor cabinet—next to the triple sec, tequila, and that bottle of peppermint schnapps someone

ATLANTA

If you're visiting **Atlanta,** check out:

The Grape (4300 Paces Ferry Rd., ☎770-803-9463). It's cozy but chic, with a friendly vibe—and no attitude whatsoever. Servers and bartenders know their vino and are only too happy to make recommendations. Oh, be sure to visit their store next door!

Wine Haven (220 Sandy Springs Circle, Suite 195, ☎404-459-0120). It's equal parts wine shop and wine bar. You'll find a diverse bunch of oenophiles here on any given night, tippling top-quality wines at great prices.

left at your place by mistake—then forget about it for months. Remember, port is a wine, even though it's more potent than most! Store it on its side in a cool place as you would any other red wine, and serve it at a reasonably cool room temperature, around 65 degrees.

Traditionally, port is served as an after-dinner drink with dessert. Never, ever pour yourself a full glass of port (or any dessert wine, for that matter)! Dessert wines are meant to be consumed in very, very small quantities for a good reason: Their alcohol level is much higher than the level in table wines. (Our friend Rusty likes to drink port straight from the bottle—but please, girls, don't follow his lead! Drink responsibly.) The sugar from any accompanying dessert will transport alcohol into your bloodstream more

Every wine has its own distinct personality—just like people. In a quandary over what wine to serve someone? Take some hints from the stars!

* Status-driven **Capricorn**: Vintage Champagne, of course.
* Lively, accomplished self-starter **Aquarius**: Try a bright, juicy Tempranillo from Spain.
* Sensual, soulful **Pisces**: Rosé's soft blush color mirrors your dreamy personality.
* Brooding, passionate **Scorpio**: Let a rich, earthy Cab stir your senses.
* The feisty ram **Aries**! You're impatient, impetuous, and bold. You'll love the near effervescence and striking scent of a Gewürztraminer.
* You're all about the good life, **Taurus**. Splurge on a great bottle of LBV port; perfect for snuggling up with your man on a chilly February night.
* You're double trouble, **Gemini**. On the one hand, you'll love a sharp, snappy Sauvignon Blanc—but your softer side will love to sip a smooth, tropically-fruity-yet-sassy Viognier.
* Intense, sensitive **Cancer**: There's nothing "light bodied" about you. Try a rich Malbec from Argentina, redolent of chocolate and tobacco. (Mmm, sinful!)
* Look-at-me **Leo**: You want attention, Leo? Well, you've met your match in a bursting-with-berries Zinfandel.
* Organized, practical **Virgo**: A good Cabernet Franc is essential! Invest in a good one from the Loire Valley.
* Worldly, exacting, and always-in-the-know **Libra**: You'll love earthy, spicy Zweigelt from Austria.
* Enthusiastic, gregarious **Sagittarius**: You'll try anything once!

quickly. Drinking a couple glasses of dessert wine with that slice of flourless chocolate cake will pack as much punch as drinking several cocktails—so take heed. Drink dessert wines in moderate quantities. They'll taste better when you know they won't give you a hangover. Cheers!

Historically, port is a *digestif* (French for "after-dinner drink"). But why stick with the status quo? We think you can drink port just about any time of day—after a long lunch, in the middle of a cool autumn afternoon, as a nightcap when you and a certain someone have arranged a rendezvous. (Don't try port with breakfast or brunch, though. Port's wonderful, but it's a little much for the first thing in the morning!)

Whenever you choose to sip it, you should serve yourself (and others!) only a couple ounces at a time. Skip those tiny dessert-wine glasses. Stick with regular-size wineglasses (or brandy snifters, if you happen to have them), so you can swirl the port around in your glass, allowing it to aerate and release its incredible aromas.

Port might be aged for ten, even twenty or more years, but that doesn't mean you should keep it around for that long! After you open a bottle, finish it in less than three weeks if you can.

Yes, You Can Drink It with Chocolate!

And now, ladies, the moment we've all been waiting for. For a simple yet decadent dessert, try a couple squares of dark chocolate alongside a glass of port. We're sure you'll be pleasantly surprised! It's just the thing for a snowy winter's night, whether you're sipping solo or drinking *a deux*.

What to Eat

Of course, port's traditional partner is Stilton cheese. Never had it? If you're a fan of blue cheese, chances are you'll love it. And even if you've never had blue cheese at all outside of the eponymous salad dressing, give it a shot! Paired with port, its pungency is softened a bit, and it's absolutely delicious. Instead of dessert, lay out a cheese board at your next dinner party or vinous shindig. Serve Stilton, sweet

Dark and Decadent

We don't need to tell you how good chocolate is. Everyone knows that! But we couldn't resist giving you a couple of recommendations. Skip the waxy, cheap kind of chocolate that 's so overly sugary, it makes your teeth hurt. Spend a few more cents, and you'll never look back! Look for any kind of Ritter Sport, a fabulous German chocolate bar with different fillings; Milka, a top-notch Swiss chocolate covered with an easy-to-remember purple wrapper; and if you really feel like treating yourself, visit *www.teuscher.com* for world-class chocolate at prices to match. Of course, in a pinch, Hershey's Special Dark will always do. Forego the milk-chocolate version of any chocolate, unless you're making S'mores! Port's richness demands something that can stand up to it.

Gorgonzola, or experiment with other types of blue-veined cheese. Then add fresh fruit, dried fruit, and nuts (walnuts are a classic supporting act to port). Sure, your dessert offering of cheese isn't supersweet, but your guests will thank you for it! Plus, you'll probably consume fewer calories eating cheese rather than, say, a heavy chocolate dessert.

What to Wear?

As little as possible if you're with your sweetie! Port warms you right up, so why bother with clothes at all? However, if you're in mixed company, don a cozy wool sweater— even better, slip on something made of angora or cashmere. Complement the ensemble with some suede boots in a rich chocolate, maroon, or ruby color. Their velvety feel and rich hue echoes port's lushness. You'll be toasty warm inside and out!

What's New Around the World?

Not much. Port certainly isn't new! It's been around since the eighteenth century, and only recently are winemakers across the world trying to create their own versions. But those ports aren't great, and we don't want to recommend them. We've had a couple tawny ports from South Africa, and while they're reasonably priced, we'd rather spend a little more and get the real thing from Portugal. Ditto with Australian examples. Of course, times are changing, so we're keeping an open mind about non-Portuguese ports, and so should you! Hard-core wine snobs might turn up their haughty noses at that blueberry port we mentioned, but it's divine. You just never know!

Oh, Sherry

Sherry is the only wine with a worse reputation than port! Just kidding. If you're imagining an old woman with a stately British accent asking her cronies if they'd take a drop of sherry—well, you're not alone. However, sherry's making a bit of a comeback. (We even had it at a winery in New Jersey!) Made mainly from the Palomino grape, it can be sweet or dry, but like all dessert wines it's always higher in alcohol than table wines. Here's a very basic primer on the main types of sherry you'll encounter in your vinous travels:

Fino. A light, dry sherry; often yeasty- and nutty-tasting.

Manzanilla. Also pale and light, it's even drier than Fino. Look for hints of crisp fruit like lemons and apples in the nose, and nuts too.

Oloroso. Slightly higher in alcohol than fino or manzanilla, but still dry. It tastes like concentrated raisins. (To each his own, but we're not big fans.)

Cream sherry. Probably one of the most well-know sherries, it's sweet, rich, and luscious, like the most decadent fruitcake imaginable.

What to Eat?

Always chill sherry right after opening it, because it spoils easily, and you should drink it within a few days. As if you needed an excuse! Like port and other dessert wines, we think you should serve it in brandy snifters or regular-sized wineglasses, so you can really make the most of sherry's incredible aromas. Fino and manzanilla sherry is great with tapas or anything salty, like nuts, olives, cured meats, Spanish sausage, and hard cheeses. If you're serving sherry—and even if you're not!—simple slices of Spanish chorizo sausage make a great appetizer.

Cream sherry is fantastic with white chocolate. (Who'd have thought?) Oh, and it's also wonderful with all sorts of bread pudding. (Another throwback to its glory days in England!) If you ever eat at a restaurant that serves bread pudding—or one of its to-die-for variations, such as chocolate chip bread pudding or banana bread pudding—be sure to order a glass of cream sherry! Otherwise, we save cream sherry for a once- or twice-a-year treat, on white-chocolate-appropriate holidays such Valentine's Day or our birthdays, of course!).

Sweet or dry, sherry's always got a kick, and both varieties match so well with decadent, "bad for you yet tastes so good" eats!

What to Wear?

Full British army regalia. Just kidding. If you're sipping sherry, you're probably in the mood to go all out. You don't usually sport short skirts? Don one today! You'll have the confidence to carry it off. Top it with a long-sleeved tee if you feel naked. Or if you're a wild child in the first place, take your glam in a different direction. Megan wears all black, all the time, so when she feels like going nuts, adding just a touch of color is a step in the right direction! Then grab a glass of sherry and indulge. Once in a while, it's good for you!

How Sweet It Is—Other Dessert Wines

What are dessert wines? They're not port, they're not sherry, so what are they? They're damn good! (We tend to get a bit overexcited just talking about them.) Dessert wines are wines with more sugar and less water than your average table wine. This makes them taste sweet, and they'll feel thick, luxurious, and viscous in your mouth. Some dessert wines are known as late-harvest wines. That means the grapes they were made from were left on the vine for an extra couple of months, almost until they became raisins, thus making their sugar levels superhigh. (Think about how a raisin tastes much sweeter than a grape.) So the juice pressed from these grapes is very thick, rich, and sugary. Yum!

Grapes can become raisin-y sweet in another way, though. Sometimes, as grapes ripen, a fungus or "rot" will appear on them. Sounds gross, no? Well, get ready for this: Unlike athlete's foot or those nasty 'shrooms growing in your front yard, this fungus is actually a *good* thing. Nicknamed "noble rot," it has an effect similar to leaving the grapes on the vines for a long time. The fungus turns grapes nearly into raisins, concentrating the sugar and leaving a sweet, thick juice.

Another wine-snobby fact: Nobly rotted grapes are used to make the famous, sweet wines of Sauternes. Although we skip Sauternes in this book—Sauternes require a whole book of their own, practically—if you fall in love with sweet wines, you might want to investigate them as well.

Though traditional wisdom claims you should never pair dessert wines with dinner, many "new school" wine professionals take a contrarian's viewpoint. Many sweet wines have higher levels of acidity, which is very complementary with rich food. In addition, the sweetness of a wine can balance the saltiness of a food, which is why port is such a lovely match with Stilton as is Sauternes with Roquefort. Try fino and manzanilla sherries with anything deep fried (wait till tomorrow to start that low-carb diet!), such as fried calamari or tempura dishes. These wines are also delicious with pasta that's prepared with cheese (but without tomato sauce) and fish cooked just about any

Good Things Come in Small Packages

Why do so many dessert wines come in half bottles? No, it's not (necessarily) a conspiracy to charge you more money for less wine. It's because dessert wines are drunk in much smaller quantities than table wine, so you'll finish the bottle more slowly. And you wouldn't want to leave a bottle of good wine, dessert or other, open for more than a couple days, because it'll spoil. Half bottles are the solution! (And they're so cute.)

way. Or, if you're more in the mood for snacking, try them alongside a few slices of rich cheese, like Brie or Camembert. Same with lightly sweet sparkling wines, like Moscato d'Asti. Port, on the other hand, really does go best with rich cheeses, particularly moldy ones. As always, let your palate and personal taste be your guide.

Ice Wine: Dessert Wine of Divas

Doesn't the very idea of ice wine sound sexy to you? It does to us! Ice wine is not made from ice, as the name would suggest. It's made from frozen grapes. In cold climates such as Germany, Austria, Canada, and upstate New York, the grapes actually freeze right on the vines before they're harvested. The grapes undergo a succession of freezes and thaws until the first deep frost when the grapes are finally harvested. By then the frozen grapes have lost most of their water, and their juice is concentrated and very high in sugar. The grapes are quickly pressed before they thaw so the concentrate does not become diluted. The process produces a juice rich in flavor and high in sugar. Because of the time and work involved in making ice wine, it is produced in small quantities and is relatively expensive (as much as $100 a half bottle, if not more!). But not all ice wine will snap your wallet in two. With a little reconnaissance, you can find good versions for under $20 per half bottle. And remember, you're not drinking a couple of six-ounce glasses of ice wine with dinner, as you would with table wine. So splurge on a bottle next time you want to toast yourself or someone special!

Ice wine is often made from the Riesling grape or from the Vidal grape (a lesser-known variety used only for sweet wines). It sports flavors and scents of peach, melon, apricot, even tropical fruits, and produces a deep golden color, the color of late summer sunshine. Swirl the Riesling ice wine around in your glass and you'll see that it's viscous, almost thick. You'll see examples from around $15 per half bottle to well over $50. We err on the side of cheapness, and so should you, till you're an expert on the stuff. If you find a cheaper bottle from upstate New York, grab it—we've never had a bad one.

ᏰᎧ CHICAGO ᏰᎧ

Visiting the windy city? Imbibe fabulous wines and enjoy decadent fare at **Chicago**'s wine-focused bars and restaurants:

At **Bin 36** (333 N. Dearborn St., ☎312-755-9463), top-notch Mediterranean/American food accompanies an amazing selection of vino in a festive, airy, classy-yet-casual setting. Try one of its many flights, which are selections of three 2-ounce glasses of wine!

Bring your appetite to **Webster's Wine Bar** (1480 West Webster St., ☎773-868-0608), where you'll find both upscale bar nibbles and a wide, thoughtful wine selection at great prices. And the best part is, the affable bartenders are always happy to chat about their passion: wine.

What to Eat?

We like to drink ice wine on its own, without any dessert at all. It's almost like candy itself, so you don't really need anything else that's too sweet. If you want to, pair it with something that's not sweet, so you're not overwhelmed by sugar. Try ice wine with strawberries and homemade, unsweetened whipped cream—an easy summertime dessert!

What to Wear?

If you're drinking ice wine, chances are you're not an ice queen! Ice wine is such a treat, we like to savor every sip, so when we enjoy it, we're probably not rushing out to go dancing. At least, not yet! A crushed-velvet pink tee is the perfect mate to a glass of ice wine. It's a snap to pair the tee with low-rise jeans—casual, yet cool. You might also want to pick out some pieces with low-key shimmer in the fabric, but nothing too gauche!

What's Hot Around the World

Just about every country in the world produces sweet wines. Well, we just love every wine we've had that's made from the Muscat grape. Sweet wines made from Muscat (Moscato in Italy) don't have that raisin-y quality that characterizes some ports and dessert wines. Instead, Muscat is highly fragrant, smelling like oranges, orange blossoms, peach blossoms, and other exotic fruits and flowers. So if you'd like something lighter and that raisin taste bugs you, sweet wines made from Muscat won't let you down. A few countries that make good, relatively reasonably priced Muscat-based wines are Australia, Italy, and the United States.

And if you ever see a late-harvest Zinfandel, snap it up. It's not easy to come by, but it tastes like a grown-up version of raspberry jam eaten straight out of the jar, with a dash of fresh-berry taste—think red cherries, black currants—to boot. Prices vary, but you'll be able to find one for around $20.

If you're a Downtown Girl with cash to spare, check out Tokaji (toh-KYE), a Hungarian dessert wine that's long beloved by wine aficionados, but is only now getting its just desserts (pun intended!) with the public at large. In fact, dessert may be all that you can afford because Tokaji's prices can be a bit prohibitive. This is because it's extremely difficult to produce. Technically called Tokaji Aszú, good versions can be aged for decades, even fifty years or more. We even heard of someone drinking a *seventy-five-year-old* Tokaji. While they're all sweet, Tokajis can taste very different from one another; some are fruity while others are toasty or smoky. Moral of the story? If anyone wants to give you a bottle, *by all means take it.* Hoard it and drink it yourself. If no one's stepping up to the plate, buy yourself a bottle after your next raise (or your next book deal).

What to Eat

Now, the million-dollar question: What do you eat with wines that are already so sweet? Well, the jury's out, but we say, nothing. Enjoy them on their own after a meal. Why make sweetness sweeter? If you really want to nibble something while you sip, steer yourself toward things that are not *sweet*. Biscotti and shortbread are good mates, or perhaps a very light yellow or white cake (but that's stretching it). We've even snacked on salted nuts with dessert wines, and the result was surprisingly good.

End It on a Sweet Note

Now you've got the whole scoop, girls. You know that dessert wines aren't fruit punch, and for those skeptics who turn up their noses at the mere mention of them—well, couldn't you tell them a thing or two! Dessert wines round off a meal, whether you're feasting on Chilean sea bass at a fine restaurant or simply whipping up pasta at home. We think their concentrated sweetness is a constant reminder of the good stuff in life, like your favorite memories: the first boy you ever kissed; being maid of honor at your sister's wedding and crying like a baby; that rush of joy pouring over you when you learned you got into graduate school; saying "yes" when he asked you to marry him. Like Champagne and other great sparkling wines, sweet wines are celebratory—but just a little more thoughtful.

Sure, you probably won't drink dessert wines every day. But we recommend that you drink one every week! Curl up with your sweetie and toast to each other with a glass or two of ice wine on Saturday night. Open a bottle of tawny port after a laughter-filled family dinner or when you're kicking back with the girls and remembering your good times. Dessert wines are the epitome of the phrase *la dolce vita*.

Resources

Bitten by the Wine Bug? It's hard not to fall in love with wine! Once you've started learning a little about vino, you might not be able to stop. And we don't blame you! So we've compiled a list of resources for learning more about the beverage that never goes out of style.

Wine for Dummies by Ed McCarthy and Mary Ewing-Mulligan (Wiley, 2003). Always a good reference to have on hand.

The Wine Avenger by Willie Gluckstern (Fireside, 1998). This is a wonderful, hysterically funny introduction to wine from an industry veteran. You won't find any snobbery or nonsense here. *The Wine Avenger* takes no prisoners, and it's a great read.

Wine & Spirits magazine. While you don't need to take everything you read in wine magazines as gospel truth, they are a good way to get on a first-name basis with wines you may not heard of, to generally keep up-to-date on what's new, and to just entertain yourself. *Wine & Spirits* keeps the snootiness to a minimum, and its articles are always well-written and interesting, whether you're a novice or an old pro. A $26 yearly subscription rate is not dirt cheap, but the magazine is worth a few extra bucks.

Wherever you're located, you can find out which wine-loving events are taking place near you at *www.local wineevents.com.* Covering both national and international events, this Web site is one of our favorite resources. Plus, it sports a section on wine news that'll feed your need for the latest dirt on all things wine related.

Visit the Riedel Web site at *www.riedel.com,* but let us warn you that's it's addictive! Riedel, one of the oldest and most widely renowned makers of stemware in the world, offers glasses for just about every wine you can think of. And you can learn about all of them on the site. Plus, there's news on tastings, history, and links to other Web sites that'll help keep you in the know.

We applaud the Wine Brats at *www.winebrats.org* for their mission: "Changing the face of wine." A young, hip group with chapters in most major U.S. cities, it's getting twenty- and thirty-somethings excited about wine—with zero toler-ance for snootiness. Becoming a member is free, and you'll get e-mails when there's an event in your area.

Want to know more about French wine? Check out *www. terroir-france.com/theclub/news.htm,* which compiles news about French wines from lots of different sources around the world. It offers one-stop shopping for everything you need to know about *vin*.

Even if you don't live in the New York area, check out the Web site for Astor Wines & Spirits at *www.astoruncorked.com*. If Astor doesn't have a wine, it doesn't exist! Okay, so maybe that's a bit of a stretch, but Astor's comprehensive site lets you search for just about any wine under the sun. Be sure to take advantage of its food-pairing tool—one click, and you'll get recommendations for what to eat with your fave bottle of vino. Of course, if you're ever in New York City, stop by; chances are you'll stumble onto a free tasting of something great, and Astor's knowledgeable staff will answer any questions in a flash.

And be sure to check out your local universities; many of them have wine education classes at reasonable prices. And many wine shops and liquor stores offer free tastings or pay-as-you-go classes on wine. Both options offer are a great way to expand your vinous horizons!

Index

dessert wines, 3, 68, 153–170;
food with, 160–161, 163,
165–166, 168, 169–170; ice
wine, 166–168; port, 154–
162; sherry, 162–164
DOC (restaurant), 30
dry wines, 11, 35–36

E

Eiswein, 3
Enoteca, 51
entertaining, 79–81, 142,
149–150

F

Falanghina, 60
Finale, 51
Fleming's Prime Steakhouse and
Wine Bar, 106
foil cutters, 14
food, 110; choosing wine for,
28–31; with dessert wines,
160–161, 163, 165–166, 168,
169–170; with red wine, 88,
90–91, 93, 94, 96, 100, 101,
104, 110; with rosé wines,
117–118; with sparkling wine,
143; with white wine, 42, 48,
49, 53, 57, 59, 60, 62, 66,
69, 78
fortified wines, 3. *See* dessert
wines
French wines, 61–63, 105–107,
122–123, 146–147
Furmint wines, 69
Fuzzy Bunny, 140

G

Gamay, 95–97
German wines, 52–53, 63–65, 71,
112–113

Gewürztraminer, 52–53, 71
glasses, 12–13, 75
Grape, The, 157
grapes, frozen, 18
Graves wines, 61
Greek wines, 69–70, 121
Grüner Veltliner, 53–54, 64–65

H

hangover cures, 27, 109, 134
hostess tips, 81
Hungarian wines, 68–69, 121–
122, 169

I

ice wine, 166–168
Impromptu Wine and Art Bar, 72
Irsai Olivér, 69
Italian wines, 58–61, 98–99, 101,
104–105, 145

J

Japanese wines, 77–78

K

Kaspar's Restaurant and Wine
Bar, 72
Kir Royale, 19

L

label removers, 15
London Wine Bar, 122
Los Angeles, 122

M

Malaga Tapas and Bar, 106
Malbec, 101, 104, 111
Merlot, 84–86, 111